The Art of Hospitality

Also Available

The Art of Hospitality Companion Book
978-1-7910-3319-4 Print
978-1-7910-3322-4 eBook

More Books by Yvonne Gentile

The Greeter and Usher Handbook

Serving from the Heart (with Carol Cartmill)

Leadership Essentials (with Carol Cartmill)

Leadership from the Heart (with Carol Cartmill)

More Books by Debi Nixon

Catch (with Adam Hamilton)

YVONNE GENTILE & DEBI NIXON

THE ART OF
HOSPITALITY

A Practical Guide for a

Ministry of Radical Welcome

Abingdon Press

Nashville

THE ART OF HOSPITALITY, REVISED EDITION

A PRACTICAL GUIDE FOR A MINISTRY OF RADICAL WELCOME

Library of Congress Control Number: 2024936569
ISBN 13: 978-1-7910-3320-0

MANUFACTURED IN THE UNITED STATES OF AMERICA

CONTENTS

CONTENTS

1

INWARD VERSUS OUTWARD CHURCHES

DEBI NIXON

We love the local church. We know its power. We both grew up in the church. It's the place where we were baptized, where we went to vacation Bible school and Sunday school as children. It's where we received our first Bibles, were confirmed, attended youth group, got married, and eventually brought our own children.

Some reading this book can relate. You grew up in the church and didn't stray far. You may now be in a church that is growing, adapting, and reaching new people and generations.

Some are in new churches preparing to launch, dreaming bold, visionary dreams as you prepare to reach a new community.

Yet, some of you who are reading may currently be in churches that are stuck, living in the past. Maybe your church is experiencing declining worship attendance, no children in Sunday school, fewer baptisms or professions of faith. Maybe you have dormant dreams, wondering if the status quo can be challenged and changed.

If that describes you and your church, we are here to tell you that, yes, it can change. It must change. The isolation of COVID-19, divisiveness, even church division, and more have had impact on the church. Yet, it's a reminder that now more than ever, the church has a vital role to play. It is time to revive dreams, ignite passions, and start a movement—a revival of the heart that breaks the hold of the status quo. It is time for a new vision to see the community through the eyes of Jesus. Jesus was outwardly focused, always giving his attention to the marginalized, the outcast, those in need, those with questions of faith. That kind of outward focus has the power to transform you and your church, and it is the path Jesus calls us to travel. The central message of Jesus was his proclamation of the kingdom of God. His message challenged the status quo, particularly the rigid church leaders who had different ideas, different standards. He awakened people to a new reality and ignited a movement. And as Jesus proclaimed this message, he invited others to join him.

> *As Jesus walked alongside the Galilee Sea, he saw two brothers, Simon, who is called Peter, and Andrew, throwing fishing nets into the sea, because they were fishermen. "Come, follow, me," he said, "and I'll show you how to fish for people."*
>
> *(Matthew 4:18-19)*

Imagine Jesus saying, "You've been fishing for fish your whole lives. You are pretty good at fishing, and now I need you. Follow me, join me in this world-changing, status-quo-breaking movement, and I'll make you fish for people." What a mind-blowing message that must have been for these first disciples. They had to choose to leave behind much of what they knew to experience something new. Yet, they responded boldly and left everything to join in this movement.

Jesus was starting a movement. And we are invited into this movement today! The church is called to this kingdom work of being ambassadors, proclaiming the good news of Jesus to others. This is our Great Commission.

But how? Are we willing to have our assumptions of how to do church, our expectations, and our comforts challenged, laying them aside so we can be a part of this movement?

The Art of Hospitality is not a book written only to help a church grow. While our hope is that the messages, ideas, and tools provided are helpful in your planning for growth, this book comes from a restless passion and calling to see every local church relentlessly outwardly focused, yielded to the call of Jesus to be fishers of people. That's a big vision, and it's the heart that compels us to write this book.

While there are many strategies for achieving this vision, this book will focus on a few of the principles, practices, and tools used at the church where we serve, Resurrection, A United Methodist Church. We are a multisite church located in the Kansas City area, including a strong, growing TV and online congregation.

Not everything will work in your context exactly the way it works for us, but if you are open, we believe you will find ideas that work in your setting.

Inward Focus

The Church of the Resurrection began in 1990 with four people and a dream. From the beginning, our senior pastor, Adam Hamilton, was clear that God was calling this church to reach nonreligious and nominally religious people. The church was not focused on reaching those who were already attending church in the community, but instead on reaching those who had no church home and were not actively engaged in growing in their faith. That passion is still the driving force behind the church today as we have become a church of over 23,000 members worshipping in multiple locations across the Kansas City community. A simple yet powerful purpose statement keeps this passion always before us:

> Our purpose is to build a Christian community where nonreligious and nominally religious people are becoming deeply committed Christians.

Our purpose statement is prominently visible at each of our locations as you enter the building. It serves as a reminder that our purpose statement drives everything we do. It drives the sermons preached, the style of worship, the ministries and programs offered. We ask that every meeting agenda has the purpose statement printed at the top as a reminder that every decision made by our trustees, our finance committee, our women's ministry team, our children's team, and so on, should help us relentlessly pursue this purpose.

That purpose has guided us from the outset. In October of 1990, at the very first worship service of Church of the Resurrection, the young pastor of this church plant, Adam Hamilton, said in his sermon, "We're going to be a church focused on people outside of our doors. We're going to be more concerned about nonreligious and nominally religious people than on ourselves." For those in attendance that day, there was deep passion and excitement around this mission.

And then it happened.

Some months later, during a meeting of the leadership team, one of the charter members said, "Pastor Adam, I love our church the size we are now. I love how close we are. I hope we never get any bigger than this." As Adam looked around the room, he noticed other leaders nodding their heads in gleeful agreement.

The leaders were saying, "Look at how we have grown since we first started. Isn't it wonderful how close we are? We are connected and know each person by name. Let's not get any larger or we will lose this sense of closeness."

Adam thought, *How did this happen?*

Just a few months earlier he had preached about our mission, had given us a compelling vision of reaching those outside our doors. Yet in just those few short months, the church was turning inward, focusing on the comfort and concerns of those on the inside.

Has this happened in your church as well? Perhaps you have discovered, as we have, how easy it is to become so close and comfortable with those on the inside of the walls of the church that we unintentionally lose concern for those outside. It's not that we don't want to reach new people. It's that we become comfortable, without realizing our comfort begins to build barriers that keep other people out. The primary unspoken question inwardly focused churches often ask is:

> What can we do, or what can the church do, to make us (me) more comfortable?

What's interesting is that most often, we don't recognize that we are this church or, if we do recognize it, won't admit that we are inwardly focused. We think we are friendly enough. We often defend our friendliness while ignoring the fact that visitors cannot find a place within our community. In reality, most everything the church does is designed for the benefit and comfort of the members, and we invite new people into "what we are already doing for ourselves."

We say that we want to grow and that we want nonreligious and nominally religious people to experience God in our churches. But our actions don't always match our words. We want to grow, but we don't want to give up our seats. We want to welcome younger people, but we don't want to change the style or time of worship. Jesus calls us to reach deeper as his ambassadors, to be fishers of people, but a church that is focused on itself begins to lose its potential in the wider community to reach new people.

Has this happened in your church?

We love those we know, to the exclusion of those we don't know. Our actions and our inward focus create barriers we simply don't see.

A mother at our church shared the story of her daughter who went away to college and attempted to get connected in a local congregation. The daughter took the initiative and visited several local churches. Most never noticed she was there. There was no welcome, no follow-up. She felt invisible. While a few churches did notice she was there, she was treated like an outsider. Eventually, she simply gave up. Through tears the mother shared that her daughter has yet to find her way back to the church. Could this have been your church? Could this happen to your daughter?

An idiom you may have heard is, "you need to take off your blinders." It comes from when blinders are put on the bridle of a horse to block their side view to keep them focused on only going in one direction. How many of our churches have on blinders that need to be removed? Blinders that keep us from seeing around us, from seeing the needs of others. Most churches likely do not recognize they are inward focused. It sneaks up on us. It blinds us.

5

If your church is not reaching and retaining new people, it is possible that some inwardly focused barriers exist. Taking off the blinders is hard. It requires us to admit that we struggle with seeking our own comfort first. It may require that we make some changes, and changes can be hard.

There are certain signs of an inward-focused church, and learning to recognize these characteristics can help us see whether and to what extent our church is inwardly focused. Thom Rainer, in his extensive research and survey of churches, found the following ten common traits among inwardly focused churches.

1. **Worship wars.** Inwardly focused churches experience members who demand that the order of worship and their preferred style of music take precedence over expressions and styles that might connect with unchurched people.

2. **Prolonged minutiae meetings.** Committee meetings focus on inconsequential items, while focus on vision and strategy to reach new people and meet the needs of the community are rarely the topics of discussion.

3. **Facility focus.** A top priority of the church is keeping the building, furniture, and grounds intact as is.

4. **Program driven.** Programs are only focused on the desires and interest of the church's members, so no margin of time, budget, or building resources is available to focus on starting new ministry that meets the needs of the community.

5. **Inwardly focused budget.** "A disproportionate share of the budget is used to meet the needs and comforts of the members instead of reaching beyond the walls of the church."

6. **Inordinate demands for pastoral care.** "All church members deserve care and concern, especially in times of need and crisis. Problems develop, however, when church

members have unreasonable expectations for even minor matters."

7. **Attitudes of entitlement.** "This issue could be a catch-all for many of the points named here. The overarching attitude is one of demanding and having a sense of deserving special treatment."

8. **Greater concern about change than about the gospel.** Change is hard for all, but when needed change meets resistance from members it becomes a barrier to participating in the work of sharing the gospel.

9. **Anger and hostility.** Some members' constant opposition toward church staff or other members can be felt throughout the church.

10. **Evangelistic apathy.** "Very few members [invite others or] share their faith on a regular basis."[1]

During the writing of this book, a local church leader called us seeking advice. The church had committed to explore some of the action steps recommended in this book. After completing the study, some of the congregants declared that they were not interested in growing and didn't want to change. For example, the church was invited to have each member sit in a different seat on the following weekend, just to experience something new. This challenge was met with great ire, and future discussions abruptly ended. Change meant they had to give up too much. They were content with maintaining the status quo so that their own needs could be met.

The Outwardly Focused Church

You may read this with some disbelief, but let's be honest: every church, including Church of the Resurrection, will naturally tend to be inwardly focused. This is the human condition. We each have a predisposition to think of ourselves first. We admit this is in ourselves. We suspect you recognize it in yourself too.

Yet, there is a second approach to consider. One where we focus outwardly on others. To be outwardly focused is to be willing to set aside our own desires and comfort so that we can be a part of the kingdom work Christ has called us to.

The question outwardly focused churches ask is:

What can we do on the inside so that those on the outside will be comfortable from the moment they arrive?

In an outwardly focused church, every ministry and program is not based on our own comfort, but instead on finding ways to connect with those on the outside of the church so they feel comfortable. It calls us to know and meet the needs of the community.

The website, way finding, preparation of the facility, design of the bulletins, hospitality, worship service, and next steps in mission and discipleship are each an important piece to help each guest feel welcomed and comfortable from the moment they encounter your church.

Far too many churches get focused on the comfort of their own members, keeping them happy so there is no tension, no conflict, no discomfort. An outwardly focused church disrupts the status quo and introduces discomfort. They have a servant mindset that champions Philippians 2:3-5: "Don't do anything for selfish purposes, but with humility think of others as better than yourselves. Instead of each person watching out for their own good, watch out for what is better for others. Adopt the attitude that was in Christ Jesus."

You can't underestimate the importance of an outwardly focused vision. Most every church that is growing has overcome inward tendencies, embracing an outwardly focused vision. That kind of vision, of course, is the heart of the gospel.

Jesus never confused his purpose. His entire ministry was about seeking and saving lost people. Luke 19:10 tells us that "the Human One came to seek and save the lost." He told parables about lost coins, lost sheep, and a lost son to reiterate his focus. We see a demonstration of his outwardly focused vision in what Jesus did. In Matthew 9:35-38 we are reminded that he not only focused on those who had already decided to follow him but also went out to the people where they were, taking the message of the good news to them.

> Jesus traveled among all the cities and villages, teaching in their synagogues, announcing the good news of the kingdom, and healing every disease and every sickness. Now when Jesus saw the crowds, he had compassion for them because they were troubled and helpless, like sheep without a shepherd. Then he said to his disciples, "The size of the harvest is bigger than you can imagine, but there are few workers. Therefore, plead with the Lord of the harvest to send out workers for his harvest."

Jesus went out. He felt compassion when he saw the crowds in the community. And he calls us, his workers, to do the same.

Do you feel compassion? Does your church feel compassion? Does your church know the needs of the community?

If we take Jesus's teaching, example, and commission seriously, as a church we must consider whether we are focused only inwardly on ourselves or outwardly on meeting and connecting with the needs of the community.

According to Thom Rainer, 90 percent of churches in North America are in decline.[2] Maybe you are in one of those churches. The good news is that this can be reversed. And adopting an outward focus is the most important step to take. Growing churches know the difference between inwardly and outwardly focused ministry, and they do something about it!

It takes leaders who remind the church why we exist. "This is where we are going," they say. "This is our mission." Growing churches are clear on their purpose. They know why they exist. They know where they are going, and they resolutely set out to work with God to accomplish that purpose.

What is the purpose of your church? Take a moment and write it down in the margin of this book. If you don't know the purpose of your church, this might be a first action step. After a major shift or crisis, as we experienced coming out of COVID-19, also provides an opportunity to reevaluate. Take time this next year to pray, discuss, and gain clarity on what God is calling your church to be and to do in your community. Having a clear sense of your purpose will help your church do the hard, necessary things to turn your focus outward and keep your attention on those outside your doors.

At the heart of the distinction between inwardly and outwardly focused church is what we are willing to do, to risk, and to give up so that we can reach those outside the church. Having an outward focus doesn't mean ignoring the needs of those in a church. There must be strategies for caring for and discipling members so that they can share their faith and be bearers of the light of Christ in the community. Being outwardly focused doesn't mean we give no thought to inward development. Some inward thinking is important and necessary, but a church that focuses most of its attention on meeting the preferences of its members will not be able to fully live into its purpose and calling to reach those on the outside. The overall focus must always be directed outward.

It's time to start a movement. It won't happen overnight, but if you commit to working on gaining clarity of your purpose, developing strategies, and casting an inspiring vision that calls your church toward an outward focus, you will find a healthy change of heart that equips and inspires the church to move outward.

You will find people who join in the great call of Christ to be co-laborers out in the harvest sharing the good news of Christ instead of demanding ministry that meets their needs. When we are outwardly focused, we can't help ourselves! This is what we do!

Maybe that young woman who hasn't been to church after going away to college will walk through your door this Sunday. Are you ready for her? The rest of this book is intended to share ideas on ways your church can go to great lengths to prepare and be ready to demonstrate extravagant welcome and hospitality to all.

Outwardly focused churches know it could be the first Sunday for someone. They are ready for that one person who might come through the door, ready to give the church or God another chance.

CHAPTER CHALLENGE

1. On pages 6–7, a list of ten common traits of inwardly focused churches is shared. Take an honest assessment of which of these you see in your own setting.

2. Transitioning from inwardly focused to outwardly focused can be hard. Our human condition wants to protect us from feeling uncomfortable. What potential changes will be the hardest for your church? for you?

3. What is the purpose statement of your church? Do most in leadership know it? Does it guide each decision made? If you don't have a purpose statement as a church, this is the place to start.

4. The mission of the church is to reach the world. Outwardly focused churches not only know this, they live into it. As you read Matthew 9:35-38, what harvest is God calling you to? Where does your leadership focus most conversations? Name friendly inward practices that prioritize members' preferences and in reality are barriers to welcoming strangers and reaching your wider harvest potential.

2

WHY HOSPITALITY MATTERS

DEBI NIXON

Have you had an experience where you walked into a business, a restaurant, or a hotel, and within seconds the first things you encountered made an immediate impression on you? Maybe you have walked into a restaurant, gotten a bad vibe, and immediately turned around and walked right back out. It might have been the smell or lack of cleanliness; it might have been the long line; it might have been the lack of customer service. Whatever it was, something in your first impression said, "I don't feel comfortable here and I am not going to stay." In contrast, maybe you have walked into a retail store with no intention of shopping, but were drawn in by an interesting display, or the welcome of a sales associate, and you found yourself not wanting to leave.

The church creates this same effect. The hospitality we demonstrate matters. Our hospitality can be a bridge that draws people in and encourages them to take a next step of faith, or it can be the barrier where individuals quickly decide to disengage.

Retail stores, restaurants, hotels, the service industry, banking...Well, let's just name it, most every business knows how important hospitality is in developing customer loyalty and engagement. Loyalty grows as customers feel cared for and valued. Yet, many people feel customer service is worse today than ever. Businesses recognize the importance of hospitality, but few take the care and time to do it well. And the same is true in the church. While we know hospitality is important, our practices are inconsistent at best, and in some cases nonexistent.

The word *hospitality* means the generous and friendly treatment of visitors and guests. Hospitality matters in the church. As the church, we are called to love visitors and guests, the stranger. In Hebrews 13:2 we read, "don't neglect to open up your homes to guests, because by doing this some have been hosts to angels without knowing it." We are commanded through scripture to demonstrate care and love to others. John 15:12 is but one example: "This is my commandment: love each other just as I have loved you."

Jesus offered hospitality during his earthly ministry. He was responsible for the most important mission in the world, yet he exercised hospitality to all while fulfilling his mission. He was never too busy, too judgmental, too weary, or too discouraged to extend hospitality to everyone he encountered. He demonstrated radical hospitality at a wedding in Cana, by turning water into wine so that all might continue to enjoy the celebration. He fed five thousand people when others encouraged him to send them away to find food in other villages. He healed a leper. He engaged in life-changing conversation with an adulterer. He welcomed women and children. He ate at a tax collector's home. Even on his way to heal someone, he stopped on the road when he felt someone else touch the hem of his robe. And he called simple fishermen to be his friends. Jesus was constantly creating environments and maximizing encounters to welcome people, heal people, engage people in conversations, moving his mission forward. Jesus's life and ministry were characterized by hospitality.

As the church, we are the living body instituted by Jesus through the power of the Holy Spirit to invite others to know, love, and serve him. That is why hospitality matters. We are the hands and feet of Christ.

You have likely heard the adage, "you only get one chance to make a first impression." It is true. First impressions matter; they are lasting. It only takes thirty seconds to make a first impression.[1] Thirty seconds! Thirty seconds to either draw people in or push them away. The first impression is when a person makes a quick mental decision about whether to explore more or to disengage.

A study conducted at New York University examined the neuroscience of how people form impressions. The study found that the amygdala, which plays a role in emotion and behavior, and the posterior cingulate cortex, which plays a role in memory, "sort information on the basis of its personal and subjective importance and summarize it into an ultimate score, a first impression." This results in forming split-second reactions or assessments on whether there is a desire to continue getting closer. The study goes on to state that "the ultimate goal is to give someone the impression that it's not only okay for the other person to get close to you, but that it would be well worth their time."[2]

Some statistics show that a guest will decide within seven minutes whether they will return to a church for a second visit.[3] As the church, we must understand what is at stake. We make first impressions on people who are trying to figure out if Jesus is worth following. The importance of making a good first impression could not be higher! Hospitality done well creates a good first impression. Hospitality helps others find a place where they feel welcomed and safe. As a church, we are creating environments where people who didn't want to go to church, now want to go to church and give God a try. When we extend radical hospitality, others discover that engaging and getting closer is absolutely worth their time. It's life transforming.

Churches that create this environment will have a strong, unrelenting value for hospitality. They recognize that hospitality demands something more, and they are willing to go above and beyond what is expected to surprise the visitor and guest.

In his book *Five Practices of Fruitful Congregations*, author Robert Schnase describes this hospitality as that place where Christians offer "the absolute utmost of themselves, their creativity, their abilities, and their energy" to welcome others into the faith. He also says that it is a "spiritual initiative, the practice of an active and genuine love, a graciousness unaffected by self-interest" so that we may receive others.[4]

The spiritual initiative of hospitality is more than friendliness. This is a hard concept for many churches to understand because they cannot see why people are not attracted to our "friendliness." Most churches are friendly, and most visitors will arrive to your church expecting some level of welcome and friendliness. Your community does not need another friendly church. There are plenty of friendly churches. Those in your community need and deserve something more from us. They need a church that values, practices, and extends radical hospitality. To reach and disciple new people, you have to go above and beyond friendliness, directing all your energy and attention toward the goal of a good first impression where a visitor or guest wants to get closer.

We represent the living Christ, and our welcome and hospitality should reflect his magnificence! We should reflect his love. Hospitality demands something more of us. It requires us to go above and beyond, stretching beyond our own comforts.

If you are looking for a small way to get started, here are two simple ideas.

- **The 3-minute rule.** Encourage each person to spend just three minutes before and after a worship service or event greeting those they do not know. People, even in a friendly congregation, naturally gravitate to visit with those they know. The result is that when visitors come, their experience too often is that no one speaks to them. So, the 3-minute rule reminds people to be intentional about greeting and getting to know others they don't know.

- **The 10-foot rule.** Encourage each person in your congregation to be attentive to the people and environment within ten feet of them. Guests do not want to be overwhelmed with welcome, so there must be a balance between great hospitality and having an entire congregation converge on someone new. The 10-foot rule ensures those in closest proximity take responsibility for introducing themselves and engaging guests with great hospitality. In addition to being responsible for noticing guests within ten feet, each congregant is also responsible for the environment by taking care of anything that may need to be addressed. Examples may be picking up trash, straightening the chairs, wiping down the countertops in the bathroom, or other aspects of the environment that contribute to a good, welcoming first impression.

These are simple rules that every church and individual within a church can follow. It takes only a commitment to do so consistently to make a big difference. Unfortunately, some inwardly focused churches just cannot get there.

We worked with a church in a rapidly growing area on an outreach campaign that resulted in dozens of first-time visitors. But no visitors returned for a second visit. Not a single one. Why? Too many inwardly focused barriers existed. The building needed updating. When visitors arrived, parking spaces closest to the building were already taken by those who arrived first—the members, not the visitors. When visitors walked in the front door, friendly congregants were busy talking and loving one another, not noticing the stranger in their midst or taking the time to welcome them. Worship was mediocre, with insider language and uninspiring music. The nursery was at the back of the church where it had been located since the 1970s. For several visitors with children, it was confusing and difficult to find. As they walked the long mazelike corridor, they passed empty adult Sunday school classrooms, one after another.

In consultation with this church, we made a few suggestions about changes to make, such as using one of the empty adult Sunday school rooms closest to the sanctuary as the nursery, positioning greeters at entry points, and adjusting language in worship to be more accessible and easier to understand for visitors. Most of the recommended changes were simply too hard, the church membership felt. It required too much change. Last year, this church closed its doors.

Talking about hospitality is not enough. It requires a decision to do things differently. Extending hospitality will require redirecting energy, focus, and resources. It most likely will require change, and for some, these changes may be uncomfortable. Going above and beyond, out of a normal zone of comfort, to connect with a person one does not know for three minutes may require risk. It takes an internal motivation that comes from recognizing how important hospitality really is.

In the book *People Are the Mission*, author Danny Franks says,

> You can't effectively preach about the extravagant grace of God if your guests have had to work themselves silly to figure out where to park or which door to enter. You can't convince people of the hospitality of the gospel if no one spoke to them. And you can't talk about "going into all the world" if you're not even willing to walk across the room to meet someone new.[5]

Missing the first five to ten minutes of worship as the greeter in the parking lot or at the front door to ensure all guests, even those arriving late, are welcomed is a sacrifice. Giving up one's preferred seat in worship so that a visitor can have the best seat, likely one on the aisle, is an act of hospitality that goes above and beyond.

In 1 Peter 4:9 we read these words: "Open your homes to each other without complaining." *Without complaining*, every ministry in the church must evaluate its current effectiveness at extending hospitality, taking steps to make necessary changes that focus on the visitor, the stranger. Every program, outreach event, communication, bulletin, signage, facility appearance, website, and handshake are all extensions of hospitality representing Jesus.

Even the scripture writers knew that welcoming strangers was hard. Our human condition draws us to self-protection, to keep ourselves from experiencing things that are uncomfortable. This self-protection can lead to complaining, grumbling, reflected often in the common refrain "but this is the way we have always done it!" Unfortunately, a church that keeps doing things the same way over an extended period without evaluation may find that, while things inside the church have not changed, the community around them has changed, and the current ministry and programs of the church are no longer relevant or able to reach a new generation of people who are in need of the good news of the gospel.

A church that values hospitality does so in response to God's call to welcome the stranger. A church that values hospitality does so in response to God's love. Because we are loved by the God who created the universe, we can't help ourselves but to respond in love and hospitality to everyone we encounter.

Matthew 25:31-40 drives home the importance of extending this kind of love and hospitality to all whom we meet:

> *"Now when the Human One comes in his majesty and all his angels are with him, he will sit on his majestic throne. All the nations will be gathered in front of him. He will separate them from each other, just as a shepherd separates the sheep from the goats. He will put the sheep on his right side. But the goats he will put on his left.*

> *"Then the king will say to those on his right, 'Come, you who will receive good things from my Father. Inherit the kingdom that was prepared for you before the world began. I was hungry and you gave me food to eat. I was thirsty and you gave me a drink. I was a stranger and you welcomed me. I was naked and you gave me clothes to wear. I was sick and you took care of me. I was in prison and you visited me.'*

> *"Then those who are righteous will reply to him, 'Lord, when did we see you hungry and feed you, or thirsty and give you a drink? When did we see you as a stranger and welcome you, or naked*

and give you clothes to wear? When did we see you sick or in prison and visit you?'

"Then the king will reply to them, 'I assure you that when you have done it for one of the least of these brothers and sisters of mine, you have done it for me.'"

When we welcome the stranger, we welcome Christ! Hospitality matters. It creates a good first impression and opens the door for people to draw closer and experience the good news of Jesus. We can attest to the power of hospitality to reach new people for Christ.

The church where we serve is one church worshipping in multiple locations across the Kansas City area. One of our locations is in the heart of the city. Our location pastor shared the story of a man released from prison, living in a halfway house, who visited our church on the first weekend he was released. The man shared that his only goal that Sunday morning was to simply find a church where he could get a bulletin that he could take back to the halfway house as evidence he had been to church. He had no intention of staying for worship. His clothes were dirty, and he was still wearing the orange prison-issued shower shoes on his feet. His plan was to enter the church, get a bulletin, and wander the city streets for a few hours by himself, returning to the halfway house with the bulletin in hand.

Something happened when the man arrived at our downtown location that day. He was greeted by someone at the door who looked him in the eye and offered him a cup of coffee. An usher helped him find a seat, and although he had the required bulletin in his hand, something compelled him to stay for just a few more minutes. The music started, drawing him in. And then it came time for the greeting. In that moment, he experienced human touch for the first time in years, through a simple handshake and word of welcome. He had been seen. He mattered. He met Christ through acts of hospitality, practiced by individuals who can't help themselves but extend it out of their love for Christ.

Visitors to your church may not remember any points of the sermon, the words to the music, the prayer, or the opportunities offered in the announcements, but they will remember how your church made them feel. They will remember each moment of the hospitality they received.

When a church decides to invest in hospitality united by God's love, enabling the congregation to reach more people with the message that they truly matter, the church becomes a force for good. And this is an investment that will outlast all of us. The community will be transformed, impacting generations into the future.

Hospitality requires us to love loving strangers. We are the hands and feet of Christ, participants in what Christ continues to do in us and through us in our community. The visitor you welcome this weekend might represent years of praying by a family member or friend. As we read in chapter 1, there is a mother praying daily for her daughter to return to church. She might walk through your door this Sunday.

CHAPTER CHALLENGE

1. Reflect on a time when you have been in a social, business, or ministry setting. How did you feel? What dynamics of the environment made you feel this way?

2. Close your eyes with a timer for 30 seconds. When someone comes to your church for the first time, what will they experience during those 30 seconds? Imagine their encounter at your website site, parking lot, front door, lobby, children's area, sanctuary. What is their first experience?

3. Scripture mandates us to practice hospitality. How do you define the difference between radical hospitality and friendliness so we can welcome the strangers among us?

4. Name action steps to institute and train leaders and then members to practice and live into the 3-minute and 10-foot rule.

3

THE PRINCIPLES OF HOSPITALITY

YVONNE GENTILE

Have you ever been somewhere where you didn't feel welcome? I worked in corporate retail for thirty years before joining the staff at Church of the Resurrection. In 1994, I moved to Kansas City for a job with a national retailer headquartered there while my family stayed behind in Georgia until we sold our house six months later.

I arrived at the office my first day a little anxious. I had left a company I'd worked with for fourteen years, and I didn't know anyone in the entire city. I was the first person hired from outside the company into the corporate office. My teammates didn't go out of their way to make me feel welcome. They would respond politely if I asked them a question, but I often felt a bit left out in conversation because they had a shared history and common language that I wasn't part of and didn't understand. They went to lunch together and sometimes forgot to invite me. Not only had that team become inwardly focused, they also, knowingly or not, resented my intrusion into their comfortable circle.

Within a week or so, I got frustrated and began going into other departments to meet people and invite them to lunch. In time, my teammates in my own department accepted me and expanded their circle to include me, but it was a hard few months. That experience taught me the importance of first impressions and making people feel welcome. I may have been the first person hired from outside the company, but I wasn't the last. I made it my responsibility to welcome each new hire who came after me. I took them to lunch on their first day, tried to anticipate and answer their questions, translated the insider language when it came up, helped them adjust to the company culture, and invited them to my house for holiday dinners. Lest you start thinking that was a big favor, I should tell you that I'm not a great cook. I may have served Kraft macaroni and cheese to one guest at Thanksgiving, only to find out after the fact that she was a gourmet cook. My goal was simply to make sure each one had a smoother transition than I had. This was my first real connection to the power of intentional hospitality.

John Pavlovitz wrote this about hospitality in his book *A Bigger Table*:

> Hospitality ascribes value to people. It declares them worth welcoming. It disarms them by easing the fears that past rejection has yielded and lets them know that this place is different. And once people realize that they are received with joy, they begin to rest in it. They breathe again.[1]

Take a moment and read that again: "Hospitality ascribes value to people....They begin to rest in it. They breathe again." When people realize they're welcomed, they begin to breathe again. This makes me think of the Hebrew word *Ruach*, breath, wind, or spirit. When we do hospitality with excellence, we create an opening for the Holy Spirit to work. We open the doorway to life change.

As church leaders, regardless of the role we serve in, we are all responsible for hospitality. Whether you are clergy, staff, or a volunteer, you play a role in making people feel welcome. Every conversation you have, every action you take, either brings people closer to God or pushes them farther away.

As we saw in chapter 2, first impressions matter because people *do* judge a book by its cover. People come to a church for the first time with hopes and fears, questions and concerns. They feel a need that they hope the church may be able to meet. They have a narrative in their minds of what they anticipate it will be like. Most of the time, they're nervous and feel truly awkward. If they've been hurt by a church or other Christians before, they're skeptical and halfway expecting more of the same. They're stepping into the unknown the first time they visit.

Remember, it only takes guests thirty seconds to form a first impression, and they'll decide within seven to ten minutes whether or not they'll return to that church a second time.[2] That's long before worship has begun or the preacher has a chance to deliver his or her message. And first-time guests will talk about their first experience at your church eight to fifteen times—more often if it's a bad experience. Can you see how important it is that we create a great first impression? Lots of people telling stories about their first experience impact our church's reputation in the community—positive or negative.

Guests come hoping to meet God, but sometimes they only meet us—and we can get in the way of them encountering God. If we provide a poor experience and welcome on the front end as guests arrive, then the task of our leaders changes from communicating a life-transforming message to overcoming the negative perceptions that we have unintentionally reinforced as our guests arrived.

For non-Christians to even get to the place where they want this is a big deal. Guests come to church because someone's dragged them here, or because they've started a family and they think they "should," or because they are in a place of crisis—a devastating diagnosis, a job loss, or simply a feeling of something missing. They come through our doors with preconceived notions of what Christians are like: cliquish, judgmental, closed-minded. Our job is to remove every possible obstacle from their path to faith. We do that by demonstrating exceptional hospitality.

We've been passionate and intentional about radical hospitality at Resurrection since we began, but we don't get it right every time, and neither will you. It is a value we continually aspire to and work toward. Excellence in hospitality transcends worship style, church size, and denomination, but we all need to evaluate regularly what we're doing to see what we can improve, because there is always room for improvement.

We recently heard a story from Amber, who is on our staff team, about an experience her husband, Will, had in worship.

I wanted to reach out to you about an experience my husband had in the 9:15 church service on Sunday, July 21. On third Sundays I volunteer in KiDSCOR [our children's ministry] and he attends the service by himself. When we got back in the car that morning he told me that he was standing in the entryway, inside the sanctuary, looking for a seat when he overheard one of the women volunteers say to the other one, "that person over there is giving me the creeps," and look in his direction. He felt very embarrassed and uncomfortable. He told me, "I wanted to tell them, I am here with my family, but they just aren't here with me."

This broke my heart on many levels because he is so dear to me and I know he has the best heart. He is 6'2" and not small. He is a sergeant at the Johnson County Sheriff's office so sometimes he will hold himself in an on-guard manner even when not at work and he doesn't smile a lot around strangers. He is on the security team at our church, but he hasn't been actively serving recently. He said he would rather be serving with security when I am volunteering because when he attends by himself, he doesn't always feel welcome.

Ouch! We have to do better than this. We share this story to show that we can and do get hospitality wrong. But hospitality remains a value for us, something we continue to pursue and try to improve.

Radical Hospitality

What does exceptional hospitality look like in practice?

At Resurrection, we often refer to exceptional hospitality as radical hospitality. We define radical hospitality as hospitality that goes beyond being friendly; it is welcoming guests with a warmth, openness, and authenticity that significantly exceeds their expectations. It is intentional hospitality that surprises and delights people by making them feel noticed, giving them personal attention, and providing excellent follow-through. It is hospitality that makes guests feel so welcome they want to return again and again.

To consistently exceed guests' expectations, we will likely have to adopt new behaviors—to go out of our comfort zone to make our guests feel comfortable. Radical hospitality creates a feeling of being comfortable, accepted, and valued—a memorable moment that people want to repeat. Friendliness is nice, but it doesn't really create a *feeling* that people will remember. Maya Angelou is often attributed with saying, "People will forget what you said, people will forget what you did, but people will never forget how you made them feel." **Guests don't come back to our churches because of what we do but because of how we make them feel.**

The difference between friendliness and radical hospitality is intentionality. We all learned a lot about intentionality during COVID-19. Suddenly, hospitality meant keeping a safe distance rather than offering a handshake; it meant smiling underneath your mask. We had to adapt our methods overnight. It was a difficult season, one I'm so grateful to be on the other side of now, but it did force us to innovate and think about new ways to make people feel welcome. Many churches established online ministries in a matter of days, and in the process, we developed new systems that will take us into the future. In chapter 6, we'll discuss hospitality in digital ministry in detail.

To exceed guest expectations on a consistent basis, whether in person or online, we have to be very intentional about it, so we've developed three principles of radical hospitality to shape how we prepare for and interact with guests. These principles help us create interactions and environments where guests are open to hearing the message in prayer, song, and sermon, and want to come back again. The three principles of radical hospitality are Notice, Offer Personal Attention, and Provide Excellent Follow-Through.

Notice

The first is the principle of Notice. There is tremendous power in noticing. We cannot provide radical hospitality until we first notice. Everything that follows—all our hospitality efforts—depends on us first noticing. To notice we must be aware of our surroundings (both the physical and digital space and the people around us) and be present in the moment.

Jesus was a master of noticing. In Luke 8 we read the story of the woman who had been bleeding for twelve years. Verse 43 tells us she "had spent her entire livelihood on doctors," to no avail. This left her ostracized in her own community. As Jesus and his disciples entered the city, they faced smothering crowds. People were pressing in from all sides. Yet when the woman touched the hem of Jesus's garment and was instantly healed, Jesus noticed.

"Who touched me?" Jesus asked.

When everyone denied it, Peter said, "Master, the crowds are surrounding you and pressing in on you!" [In other words, how could you possibly notice one person touching you?]

But Jesus said, "Someone touched me. I know that power has gone out from me."

When the woman saw that she couldn't escape notice, she came trembling and fell before Jesus. In front of everyone, she explained why she had touched him and how she had been immediately healed.

"Daughter, your faith has healed you," Jesus said. "Go in peace.""

(vv. 45-48)

Most of us aren't as aware as Jesus was; we have a running monologue (or dialogue) in our minds. To be fully present, we have to press pause on what we're thinking or doing, and press play on what the person in front of us is saying or doing. The enemy of noticing is rushing. When we're rushing around, it is hard to pay attention to anything outside our immediate task. The way we often describe the principle of noticing is this: **we want to give our guests the gift of an unhurried moment.** That's why we ask our volunteers to arrive earlier than their scheduled time to serve, so they can get their assignments, needed supplies, and instructions and then be prepared to notice.

Noticing includes:

- Offering a warm greeting to each guest you encounter.
- Being on the lookout for people and environmental issues that need special attention.
- Developing a dependable system for noticing and acknowledging guests.

Let's look at each one of these more closely.

Offer a warm greeting to each guest you encounter, starting with the person right in front of you.

Everyone loves to feel welcomed, including longtime members. This starts with making eye contact and smiling warmly. Research shows that smiling improves our own mood, and our smiles makes those around us feel better too. Do you know that if you smile during a phone conversation, it warms up your voice, and the person on the other end of the line can tell you're smiling? It transforms your interaction.

This is true at church, and it's true in other areas of life as well. One of my favorite places to practice this is at a retail store. Somehow, I always manage to get into the absolute slowest checkout line. Does this ever happen to you? I'll notice the people in line ahead of me getting frustrated (and vocally taking their frustration out on the cashier by being rude). Having worked in retail, I can tell you that this makes for a miserable day at work. I make it my mission when I reach the front of the line to smile and make an encouraging comment: "Hi! Looks like you guys have been slammed. Thanks for your patience when us customers get testy." Without exception, at that point they look up, make eye contact, smile back, and their entire face lights up. As I leave, I wish them a great rest of their day. It makes my day, and I believe it makes theirs too.

Just think what a difference it would make in your mood if, one day, everyone you encountered greeted you with a smile. Imagine what a difference we could make if every staff person, volunteer, and congregant made it their mission to make eye contact and smile at the people they interact with at church. We're not advocating for fake smiles, or forced good moods, if that's not what they're feeling, but a commitment to finding opportunities to smile, nod in acknowledgment, or say hello to the people they see. It creates a sense of acceptance and welcome without actually requiring much of us at all.

Be on the lookout for people who are alone or look lost and for issues in the environment or facilities.

Do you see someone who might need assistance? Is there trash or a spill on the floor? Is there a broken piece of equipment? Is the space clean, neat, and distraction-free?

A few months ago, at the end of worship one Saturday night, Eileen, one of our ushers, noticed an older woman with a middle-aged couple that stayed in the sanctuary long after most folks had exited. Our pastors were outside the sanctuary greeting people. There was nothing noticeably wrong, but Eileen just felt as though she should have one of the pastors check on them, so we called our care pastor, Joshua, who was available at that time.

He learned that this was a mother with her son and daughter-in-law, and it was their first time in our church. They had gotten the news the day before that the mother's cancer was terminal—there were no treatment options left. Pastor Joshua spent thirty minutes with the family and made an appointment to follow up with them later. This family came to our church with a heavy burden on their hearts. They came looking for hope, for strength and encouragement. They received much-needed care because Eileen noticed them and paid attention to her instinct that they were in need.

During our Easter services last year, I was serving at our welcome desk when I noticed a couple come into the Commons, while looking up and around, like they were trying to take everything in or looking for something specific. How did I know they were new? Well, I didn't really, except for their body language. I approached them and said, "Good morning! My name's Yvonne. Can I help you find something?" They introduced themselves and said they had begun worshipping with us online during COVID-19, and that weekend was their first time to worship in person. I gave them a little tour of our location, and as we walked and talked, we discovered we had a mutual friend. When they left, they thanked me for spending time with them and said they'd be back. It was a small thing, but that personal interaction contributed to their positive experience of our church, and all I had to do was pay attention and be ready to act.

Develop a dependable system for noticing and acknowledging guests.

Some churches ask guests to stand. Others have a tent or booth outside the sanctuary where newcomers are given a gift for providing their contact information. Other churches ask guests to fill out and turn in a connect card to an usher.

There are benefits and disadvantages to all of these approaches. We received an email from a pastor at another church shortly after Christmas. She said her church had mailed a postcard inviting their community to attend a candlelight Christmas Eve service. That postcard worked, because this small church estimated that 70 percent of their attendees for their Christmas service were new people. The pastor held up the connect card, and invited people to fill it out and hand it to an usher after the service. The pastor shared that she felt she'd done a great job of encouraging people to complete and turn in the cards, but she was so disappointed. Not one new person filled out a connect card, even though the church knew they had a significant number of first-time guests. Maybe your church has great success with connect cards or something similar. Some churches invite people to fill them out and bring them to a specific location to receive a gift as a way to encourage them to participate.

Because our target audience is nonreligious and nominally religious people, we believe calling attention to them in service would make them uncomfortable. In fact, most guests prefer to wait until they've visited a few times before they let anyone know they're visiting. We want to go out of our way to make them comfortable, so we let them fly under the radar if they want, but we still have a process to notice them.

We ask everyone to register their attendance in worship. Pre-COVID-19, we used attendance notebooks, with a white pad for members and a blue pad for guests on the right side, and welcome packets on the left. Passing the notebooks was a separate element in every worship service, and it usually happened about fifteen minutes into the service. We intentionally put this element right before the sermon because people are always late! The pastor would say something very close to this from the chancel:

> I'm going to invite our ushers forward to hand you the attendance notebooks. If you're a guest with us today, I want to welcome you. We're so glad you're here. There's a welcome packet on the left-hand side for you to take with you, that provides more information about our church. Your presence here is very important to us. Please take the time to fill the attendance notebook out to let us know you were here, and pass it down the row. When it gets to the end of the row, pass it back to the beginning. As it comes to you a second time, look for the names of the people sitting on your right and left, and greet them by name after worship.

Because this was a dedicated part of the service, everyone was filling out attendance at the same time, so no one felt singled out. We asked our members to set the example by filling their side out completely. Because it was a special element of the service, and there was some peer pressure at play—the pastor told the person sitting next to you to look for your name—almost everyone filled it out. This was a pretty old-school method of taking attendance, especially with all the technology available today, but we had above 80 percent participation with that method, which we are not seeing since we moved to online attendance registration in response to COVID-19.

Once the service ended, our ushers gathered all the completed sheets and brought them back to the usher room. The blue sheets marked "this is our first visit" were held aside for our immediate follow-up processes, which we'll share later in the book.

All the sheets were picked up by volunteers by Sunday evening, who entered the information into our database. This process enabled all our follow-up processes with guests and members, which we'll discuss in chapter 7.

During COVID-19, we moved to an online attendance form. The same volunteers who used to pick up forms to enter manually now received their "lists" via email to enter into our database. One huge benefit was they weren't struggling to read people's handwriting.

In July of 2023, we installed a new database that has an integrated attendance process. The pastor instructs people to go to cor.org/next to tell us they're here, or they can text HERE to a phone number, that returns a link for them to enter their attendance. No more mass manual data entry! While we celebrate that, we are also faced with significantly lower participation rates. Roughly 58 percent of people who worship in person register their attendance. For online worshippers, that rate drops to about 35 percent (which is about the same as it was pre-COVID-19). During the pandemic, we also began to broadcast our worship services on a local TV station, and fewer than 5 percent of TV worshippers register their attendance.

We continuously look for ways to increase participation in attendance registration and have tried numerous ways of incentivizing people—a free downloadable resource, a gift, and so on. Whatever method you choose, the most important thing is to develop a system for noticing and acknowledging guests that is dependable and consistent.

Offer Personal Attention

The second principle of radical hospitality is personal attention, and it's completely dependent on making space in your life to notice. When guests receive personal attention, it's memorable. It doesn't happen often in these days of self-service and screens. How often do you call an organization that you need information from, only to be caught in a never-ending cycle of automated instructions? Have you noticed the trend at retail stores to install self-checkout lines, which means no interaction with a cashier? As our world gets more and more connected online, it seems we are also more isolated interpersonally.

In their book *The Power of Moments*, Chip and Dan Heath quote service expert Leonard Berry: "To *exceed* customer expectations and create a memorable experience, you need the behavioral and interpersonal parts of the service. You need the element of pleasant surprise. And that comes when human beings interact."[3]

People come to church and expect one of two things: to be smothered by overzealous church people, or to be just another face in the crowd. When we take the time to make them feel seen and heard as individuals, we surprise and delight them. We show personal attention in many ways, including:

- Introducing yourself and learning people's names.
- Wearing nametags and other identifying markers.
- Practicing the 10-foot rule and the 3-minute rule.
- Introducing the people you meet to others.
- Looking for opportunities to go the extra mile.
- Anticipating and fulfilling guests' needs.

These are simple practices, but they have the power to make guests feel noticed and seen through personal attention.

First, introduce yourself, and learn people's names.

Let's talk about how to introduce yourself. You don't want to ask people if they're new. You might say something like: "I'm not sure we've met. I'm Susan. How's your day going so far?" Or "Good morning! My name's Tim. It's so nice to see you!" What if you've forgotten their name? It happens to all of us. Say "Good evening! I'm Donna. I think we've met before, but your name escapes me. Would you mind reminding me of your name?" Ninety-nine percent of people are going to appreciate you asking and will not be offended by your poor memory. It happens to them too.

We recently led a group of people from our church on a trip to Egypt, to walk in the footsteps of Moses. Spending ten days together in a foreign country creates a bond. We formed deep bonds with the people on our respective buses, and a lighter connection with those who were on different buses. On the flight home, sitting in airports waiting for connecting flights, I had a great conversation about our trip experience with a woman who wasn't part of my bus group, but then we parted ways when we arrived back in Kansas City.

The following week I worshipped at one of our locations and noticed this woman was playing the keyboard and singing with the worship band. For the life of me, I could not recall her name.

When the service ended, and she was gathering her stuff, I walked up on the chancel and tapped her on the shoulder. She looked at me with a blank look on her face, so I said, "I don't know if you remember me, but I'm Yvonne, and we flew back from Egypt together." Recognition sparked in her eyes, but I still couldn't think of her name, so I simply said, "I'm sorry, I was so excited to see you up here and be able to reconnect, but I can't remember your name. Will you remind me?" She told me her name was Cindy and we proceeded to have a ten-minute conversation about our recovery from jet lag and the amazing experience we shared.

On our online services, which are pre-recorded now, rather than live streamed, we include a welcome segment, where two of our church leaders, typically people worshippers will see leading the worship service, offer a welcome (and smiles!) and introduce themselves. Then they ask people to register their attendance so we can get to know them too. We believe it helps create a sense of belonging when online attendees, who may never worship in person, begin to recognize names and faces.

If your church uses nametags, team T-shirts, or lanyards, wear them.

Nametags, T-shirts, lanyards, and other similar items are tools that help people identify you as someone who might be able to answer questions. It allows you an opportunity to introduce yourself and ask their name(s) too.

Several years ago, we purchased T-shirts for our volunteers that had a simple message: "We're Glad You're Here!" That phrase has a great deal of power. We all want to believe that someone is glad we are here. Yet the reality for many people is that's not their experience.

A few years ago, Aaron, one of our congregational care ministers, shared a story at staff chapel. A friend of his had called him on a Saturday morning and told him he was contemplating suicide. He felt rejected by his family, unaccepted and alone. Aaron told him, "I'm so glad you called me. Why don't you come to church with me tonight and then we'll go out to dinner after and talk more about it?" His friend agreed. As they approached the door, our greeter, who was wearing one of these T-shirts, warmly greeted him and said, "I'm so glad you're here." As they sat in the sanctuary, two other people came over and spoke to them, welcoming Aaron and his friend. Aaron's friend started to tear up as worship ended, and told him, "I haven't felt this accepted in a long time. Being here tonight and feeling so welcomed has given me hope to carry on."

The T-shirt not only sends that message to our guests; it's also a reminder to our volunteers and members to offer that welcome. You might be thinking, "That's great but my volunteers are never going to wear a T-shirt." We have some of those volunteers too. Our staff can even feel that way. One of our team members shared a story that changed her thinking about T-shirts. It was a couple of months after we'd moved into our sanctuary, and she'd been working every weekend, always wearing her "We're Glad You're Here!" T-shirt. As she got dressed this particular Sunday morning, she mentally groused about having to wear the T-shirt again, but she reminded herself that she needed to set an example for all our volunteers. They won't do what we ourselves aren't willing to do.

She was outside the sanctuary between services, and the space was crowded with people. Her attention was divided, responding to a congregant's question and also listening to an usher say something on her radio earpiece, when suddenly she felt a tiny hand grab two of her fingers. She looked down to see a little boy, about four years old. He looked up at her and asked, "Can you help me find my Daddy?" Our team member realized then that the T-shirt really did help our guests— big and little—know who to turn to for help.

In 2020, Resurrection launched its first kindness campaign, #LoveYourNeighbor, and had real estate signs and T-shirts printed for congregants. This has become a biannual campaign, running during October of election years, with a new theme (and new T-shirts) each year. Since that first campaign, our volunteers have preferred to wear those T-shirts when serving. They still convey a positive, welcoming message and help identify team members. We provide usher/greeter buttons and lanyards as well.

Practice the 10-foot rule and the 3-minute rule.

We introduced the 10-foot rule and the 3-minute rule in chapter 2, and these are important ways to be more welcoming to guests by giving them personal attention. To remind you, the two rules are:

- **The 10-foot rule:** Take responsibility for greeting those seated or standing within ten feet of you, especially if they're alone.
- **The 3-minute rule:** Spend at least three minutes before and after any other church activity talking to someone you don't know very well.

One weekend, I visited our Blue Springs location for worship. As I was walking up to get coffee, the man in front of me turned around, said hello, offered me the cup he had just filled, then poured another for himself. We introduced ourselves, I thanked him, and then we parted. As I sat in the sanctuary before worship, I realized he was sitting in front of me. We had a nice conversation and learned our children had some things in common. A month or two later I was back at Blue Springs, and when I walked in, the same man said, "Hello. It's good to see you again!" I could tell he recognized me but didn't remember my name. Still, how do you think that made me feel? Yes—I'm the staff person and I felt welcomed by a congregant. It felt amazing! We all like to feel welcomed.

It's also a good idea to introduce the people you meet to others you know and include them in your conversations with church friends. We look forward to seeing our friends when we come to church, and our congregations do too. The 3-minute rule and 10-foot rule are not meant to hinder opportunities to connect with those we know well. We're not suggesting you never talk to your friends but that you expand your circle, invite a new person into the conversation, and make introductions so that the new person feels included and can build connections with others.

Look for opportunities to go the extra mile.

When someone asks directions, don't just point—walk them to their desired location and make conversation along the way. Go out of your way to make things easier and more comfortable for them. To make this possible, it helps if you can position your volunteers in teams, so one can stay in place while the other person escorts the guest.

Upon joining our ministry team, Sue and Don told us about their first visit. When they arrived at the north door to our sanctuary, our greeter, Bill, opened the door for them, and they asked him, "To get to the sanctuary, do we just keep going straight?" Bill knew then that they were new and asked them to wait with him for just a moment. He recognized the couple coming toward the door behind them as regulars. He introduced them and asked the regulars if they'd show our guests to the sanctuary. They did, but first they showed the new couple around, got them a cup of coffee, and invited them to sit with them. Sue said she and Don made the decision that evening that they'd found their church home.

One family that had begun worshipping online with us during COVID-19 had filled out a prayer request for a terminally ill family member. One of our pastors, Ashley, followed up with the family and provided care to them long distance, with weekly contact. When their family member passed, they asked if Pastor Ashley could fly to them and do the funeral service. That wasn't an option at the time, so Ashley suggested they find a local pastor and offered to connect them with one in their area. Because they had been cared for so well by her, though, they really wanted to have Ashley lead the funeral. Ashley offered to preach the funeral message via Zoom, but she was sure they wouldn't want that. To her surprise, they were delighted to have a solution, and were grateful for her willingness to go above and beyond.

Anticipate and fulfill guests' needs.

Most hotels anticipate their guests' needs by providing little bottles of shampoo and lotion, soap, extra pillows, towels, and thankfully, in-room coffee makers. For churches, anticipating our guests' needs may be providing print information about the church and its ministries at the welcome desk or providing tissues during cold and flu season and coffee all year round. Some churches anticipate guests' needs by providing lotion, cough drops, and mints in their restrooms. During COVID-19, we did this by providing hand sanitizer and masks.

We have a team of volunteers who work behind the scenes throughout the week, readying our space for our guests who'll come the next weekend. They fill seatbacks with sermon note cards and offering envelopes, as well as pens, in an effort to anticipate our guests' needs. They do it knowing that they are doing sacred work by preparing our space to receive guests.

Provide Excellent Follow-Through

Our final principle is Excellent Follow-Through, and this one encompasses everything that happens after that first encounter with a guest or after we first notice an issue in our environment or facilities. John Maxwell is quoted about the impact of excellent follow-through this way: "Diligent follow-up and follow-through will set you apart from the crowd and communicate excellence."

Excellent follow-through can also be as easy as the flip side to a warm hello. Offering a warm and sincere "Goodbye! Looking forward to seeing you again!" as a guest departs concludes your encounter in a way that is just as pleasant and hospitable as it began. Here are some other ways to provide excellent follow-through in your church.

If you see a problem, own the process of finding a solution.

One of the challenges with providing excellent follow-through is that when we see a problem, we assume someone else is going to take care of it. One way to demonstrate excellent follow-through is by taking responsibility.

If you use the restroom and there's water all over the counter, grab a paper towel and wipe it up so it's dry for the next person. If you see a bulletin lying on the floor as you exit a service, pick it up. If you see someone with their arms full trying to come through the door, open it for them and offer to help carry something.

One Christmas Eve, in between our two busiest services, when we were over capacity in both the sanctuary and the Foundry worship space, we had three volunteers who went above and beyond. Our sanctuary is shaped like a large oval with a *U*-shaped lobby. On the north ends of our lobby, the hallways get narrow, and they were packed with people. Our volunteer check-in space was in the parlor, just outside the northeast hallway. A woman who had signed up to be an usher for the next service came running in, saying that the ladies' bathroom next door was running over. It was clean water, but it was starting to flood the room and head toward that hallway, where our guests were walking. We called facilities and then ran to the bathroom, where this woman and two others she had recruited were frantically throwing paper towels on the floor to keep the water from reaching our guests in the hallway. Now that it's over, we can laugh about it, but at the time, we were kind of in panic mode. We were so grateful for the action of these volunteers who saw a problem and took responsibility for finding a solution.

Search out answers to questions you can't respond to in the moment.

Searching out answers to questions you couldn't respond to in the moment and making sure the *guest receives the answer* is another example of excellent follow-through.

Several years ago, one of our volunteers, Ellen, called our office. She was serving at our Connection Point, and a woman had come in looking for a Bible she'd lost at the church a little over a month earlier. She'd been looking all over for it, and finally realized she must have lost it at church. She said it didn't have her name on it, but it was special to her because her mother had given it to her and written a special inscription inside, and her mother had recently passed away. Ellen knew that our process for lost and found items is to keep them for thirty days and then to donate them if they haven't been claimed. She asked if there was any way to track where we would have donated it to. We were uncertain but told her we'd check. Ellen was insistent that we call her back regardless of the answer so that she could respond to the guest. Amazingly, one of our mission team members remembered that we'd donated the unclaimed Bibles to a women's shelter in town that month and called the shelter. Long story short, a day later they found the Bible. When we told Ellen it had been found, she was so excited. You'd have thought it was her own precious Bible. She called the guest immediately, and we were able to get it back to her.

Finally, excellent follow-through includes intentional follow-up processes, which we'll cover in chapter 7.

Hospitality Changes Lives

When we live into the principles of radical hospitality, we give people a taste of the kingdom of God. By showing that we are anticipating and ready for guests, that they are welcomed and accepted, we become the physical manifestation of Christ's love and welcome for those who come. When we make their experience exceptionally positive, their preconceived notions about church (and Christians) are deconstructed; they're open to returning, which is the first step in a life of faith.

Your role at your church, however large or small, whether behind-the-scenes or public-facing, is critical to people experiencing a taste of God's kingdom here on earth.

When hospitality is done well, it changes lives. In April I was worshipping at our downtown location, and as I usually do, I struck up a conversation with the person sitting next to me. I asked him a question I always ask people I meet at one of our locations: "What brought you to Resurrection?" He said, "Well, at first it was the coffee. You see, nine months ago I was a drunk, living on the streets. When this church opened, word got around that they had good coffee. I'd sneak in one door, grab a cup of coffee or two, and then sneak out the door on the opposite side." I said to him, "What happened? You're not sneaking in now." And he said, "One day as I was filling up my coffee cup, a guy invited me to come inside and stay for worship. I told him I was too dirty and smelly, and he said, 'No one is too dirty and smelly. Come sit by me.' It changed my life. I decided to get sober, and I connected to a men's Bible study. I've got a place to live and a part-time job. This week I am celebrating nine months of sobriety."

I was moved to tears. I instantly thought of the parable Jesus told in Matthew 25:

> *I was hungry and you gave me food to eat. I was thirsty and you gave me a drink. I was a stranger and you welcomed me. I was naked and you gave me clothes to wear. I was sick and you took care of me. I was in prison and you visited me. (vv. 35-36)*

That man's life is different today simply because someone welcomed him in, despite his being dirty and smelly. The man who invited him inside the sanctuary noticed him, offered him personal attention, and followed through by sitting beside him, making him feel welcomed and accepted, just as he was. Dr. Amy Oden said it this way: "The deepest welcomes, often unexpected, profoundly shape our views of ourselves, of others, and of God."[4]

Before anyone decides to grow deeper in their faith, or be healed in their brokenness, or get connected in community, they first have to feel like they belong. That's true regardless of their entry point. Think through each of your ministries. Do you have greeters welcoming people during special events at your church? Does your student ministry welcome and follow up with students who come for the first time? Do your Sunday school classes welcome new people? Do you have volunteers ready to notice, offer personal attention, and provide excellent follow-through?

CHAPTER CHALLENGE

1. Evaluate how well your church currently lives into the value of exceptional hospitality. What are you doing really well? Where is there room for improvement?

2. Think about how you might introduce and implement the Principles of Hospitality at your church in order to create more intentionality around hospitality. Who can authorize you to move forward? Whose buy-in do you need for the implementation to succeed? Who can you involve who can take responsibility for some parts of the plan? How will you communicate the principles to your volunteers and congregation?

3. Identify 1-3 key actions that would produce the greatest impact on your hospitality. Invite key leaders in your church to begin to intentionally model those behaviors for your congregation. People will do what they see leaders modeling.

4

CREATING A DIGITAL FRONT DOOR

YVONNE GENTILE

One summer my husband and I, along with our two adult children, took a road trip to the Outer Banks in North Carolina to visit family. With that many adults along, we thought it might be more cost effective to rent a house rather than stay in a hotel, so I began to do some research on vacation homes for rent. I found myself automatically ruling out homes that didn't have plentiful photos or didn't provide much detail about the location and amenities provided. I carefully read the reviews written by people who had stayed in the locations I was considering.

I narrowed it down to three options: one that was a little farther from our family, but had more space and looked newer; one that was right in the middle of town and had more high-end amenities; and one that wasn't fancy, but looked comfortable, was close to family, and included not only pictures of the house and rooms inside, but also photos of the included amenities (a dock, crab pots, bicycles, a kayak, and so on). It also had detailed maps and descriptions of what was available nearby. None of the listings contained quite the same information, so I emailed the owner/property manager of each one to ask a question about that specific property.

The owner of the last property responded within five minutes, and not only answered my question but offered some additional information. The property manager of the first one, the largest and most expensive rental, responded twenty-four hours later with a form letter, referring me back to the online listing for information (where there was no answer to my specific question, or I wouldn't have needed to email). The owner of the home right in the middle of town responded a day and a half after my email, with a warning that several other people were looking at the property, and if I didn't confirm soon, I'd miss out on the opportunity to stay at their home.

As you probably guessed, I booked the house that provided lots of information online and whose owner was quick to respond. The lackluster online presence and poor responsiveness of the other properties took them out of consideration quickly. I forwarded a link to the home we'd booked to our children, who both live out of state, so they could look at the photos and description. They both began to get excited before we even left home. My daughter couldn't wait to learn how to kayak, and my son and husband began to look forward to trying out the crab pots. For me, it was the porch swing facing out toward the intercoastal waterway that I couldn't wait to use.

Our opinions and high expectations about this home and our vacation were set before we ever stepped foot on the property, based entirely on its online presence and the responsiveness of the owner. Thankfully, our vacation completely lived up to those expectations.

Radical hospitality begins long before a guest walks in the door or worships online for the first time, before any interaction takes place with a volunteer. It starts with paying attention to the details of your online presence. In a world where we Google everything and every organization has a website, you can count on guests checking you out online before they visit. Over 85 percent of first-time guests visit a church's website and social media platforms before they visit in person. That's a number that should get our attention because it means that whether you know it or not, your online presence is your front door for guests. Think about the last time you visited a business or organization you'd never been to before. You likely did some informal online research before you visited. And you formed an impression—good or bad—about that organization based on their online presence. The first impression of a website or other online presence is formed within milliseconds, based on what you see at first glance. Your goal, then, is to make sure your digital front door—your website and social media—makes an excellent first impression and provides enough information to encourage guests to visit in person.

The first step is to create a welcoming online presence. You can't afford not to, truthfully. Our culture not only increasingly turns to digital platforms for information, we are also more frequently doing it from mobile devices. For millennials and generations that follow, mobile devices are the primary internet search vehicle. They might search for a website, a Facebook page, or an Instagram or X (formerly known as Twitter) account, or all of the above.

Website

Think about your website first. Is it dynamic, working as well on a mobile device as it does on a computer (though it will look different)? According to the Pew Research Center, 90 percent of adults in the US use the internet, and roughly one in five use their phone or other mobile device exclusively (rather than a computer) to access the internet at home.[1] A mobile-friendly website is critical.

The good news is there are so many new, user-friendly tools available for website creation that you no longer need an IT department, an outside vendor, or someone who can write code in order to build a website. In fact, Resurrection's Digital Engagement Team Director, who manages all of our digital media, has never written a line of code. He recommends checking out tools like WordPress, Elementor, Square Space, and Framer, which don't require coding skills and offer a lot of online tutorials.

Is your website warm and inviting, or is it a little bland? Is it functional and easy to navigate? Is your website guest-friendly, or targeted more toward your existing congregation? Does it help guests plan for their first visit?

Your website speaks in an official capacity about your church. It is viewed as an authorized representation of the organization, and visitors to your website expect it to accurately represent who your church is and what it values.

First and foremost, your website needs to be functional.

I was preparing to speak about this topic at a conference we hosted a few years ago, and I decided to visit the website of the church where I first got connected—truly connected—as an adult. I found a very basic website, with three buttons in the center of the page: What's Happening in Our Church? (which took me to the worship schedule), What's Happening in Our Community? (which took me to a blank page), and Prayer Requests.

What would you expect if you clicked on the prayer request button? I expected to find a place where I could submit a prayer request. Instead, it took me to a page with the words to the Lord's Prayer. I visited their website again a year later, and it had been updated with fresh colors, but still had the three buttons, which still took me to the same places (except now the prayer request page said "form coming soon"). Visiting this website made me sad because it told me the church that once nurtured me was no longer thriving. In fact, today when I tried to visit that website again, I learned it no longer exists. That church has closed permanently.

We know it can be hard to keep everything on a website updated. We sometimes find broken links and outdated information on our pages too. But everything on your home page must be functional. As an official representative of your church, if your website creates a poor first impression, it's not just giving a poor first impression of the website itself, but also of the church as an organization.

Make sure your website is guest-centric and explicitly welcoming.

Rather than buttons or a ton of text, lead with an inviting image on your home page, one that feels warm and welcoming. Include an explicit message of welcome on your home page, using as few words as possible. People tend to scan text, but images have an immediate impact. The image on your home page speaks to a guest about what your church will be like. Feature images of people, not facilities. You want to show guests visually that they belong. When guests see people who look like them, their assumption is they'll be welcomed and accepted too.

Welcome *guests first* on all outward-facing marketing, including your website, rather than your members. Websites are one place where many churches easily become inward focused, featuring events, classes, and programs for members. For instance, I've seen churches whose home page says: "Don't forget to turn in your capital campaign commitment!" What message does that send to a guest?

Your regulars have other options for finding information they need, but this is a guest's ONLY method of gaining insight and information about your church before they visit. Make the information a guest needs front and center.

Communicate to your members that you're not neglecting their needs; you're simply focusing on your mission of reaching new people. Ask members to take the extra step to click deeper into the website or to scroll further down the page. Instead of featuring internal messaging on your website, communicate those messages by email or direct mail.

Use language on your website that guests can understand. Every church develops their own clever names for ministries. While these can create a sense of identity and belonging, they are quite frankly like a foreign language to guests. Randy Greene, who previously served as our digital media specialist at Resurrection, said this about catchy insider terms: "An instant of confusion is an instant of distrust, which has to be overcome later. If we minimize confusion, we minimize distrust." As an example, when Randy first came to our church and looked on our website, he saw a button for Rezlife. He assumed that was the name of our small group or life group ministry, but it's the name of our student ministry. He had to figure out what Rezlife actually was, and those moments of confusion became a barrier for him to connect with our church quickly. Now our website lists student ministry, which is clear even to unchurched people. Over the last year or so, we've gone through a process of intentionally moving away from all of those "catchy" ministry names, to terms that provide quick clarity.

We tend to use churchy words as part of our normal vernacular, often words that leave guests feeling clueless—and when they're clueless, they're not having a great experience. Words like *narthex*, *Lent*, and *Advent* aren't familiar to unchurched people. As much as possible, use clear language or include an explanation to help guests understand your terminology.

Create an easy-to-navigate transition path from online to physical space.

An in-person guest's primary concern when they check out your website is reducing their anxiety about their first visit, so make sure they can easily find information they're looking for with two to three clicks. Many churches have done this by adding a New Here, Welcome, or Visit tab that takes guests to information like:

- Service times and a description of services
- What to expect
- Information about children's programs and the nursery
- Address and photo of your building
- Information about your pastor/staff

On Resurrection's home page, a guest can get this information by clicking the Visit Resurrection button in the center of the screen. Clicking that takes you to a Plan a Visit page with a clear message of

"We're Glad You're Here!" and buttons to get more information about our locations.

Clicking a location and "learn more" takes guests to a page about the individual location, including the physical address and times of both in person and online worship services.,

One feature of our website that began during COVID-19 is the "Next" tab. It's featured as a button on our home page and on each location's page. We used to make announcements in worship and provide a separate URL or shortcut to each one, but we've consolidated that into one page, so guests and members alike know they can go there to find anything that was mentioned in worship last week. We use this shortcut to take guests to upcoming events or service opportunities we're featuring, as well as links to register attendance, sign-up for pastors' newsletters, a daily devotional, or to give.

It's important to include your address and a photo of your property, showing your primary entrance. This shouldn't necessarily be on your home page (remember, feature people, not facilities), but do make it easy to locate. That enables guests to navigate to your location and find their way inside your building more easily. I'm horrible with directions (yes, even with GPS), and I get a little nervous when I go to a new place for the first time. I always look up the location online and see if I can find a photo of the building and some landmarks nearby, so I can feel confident I'm in the right place when I arrive.

Make it easy to find information about your children's ministry.

Provide plenty of information on your website about your children's ministry, with photos showing clean, bright classrooms and happy children (note that you will need parental consent to post photos of children). Give clear instructions about the location of your children's ministry, times that programming is available (and for which age groups), and your drop-off process. If a form needs to be completed before parents can drop their kids off, give them the ability to fill that out ahead of time. Each week we have several families who fill this form out before they arrive, but more often the family arrives without having done so and we help them complete the form onsite. Informing them on the website that we have a form that needs to be filled out at least gives them awareness in advance that their first check-in might take a few minutes. Here's a paragraph from our website as an example:

> What to expect: You will be welcomed with a smile as our team helps you get checked in. We recommend arriving 20 minutes before the service starts to complete our check-in form capturing critical parent/guardian info and any special needs your child may have. You can fill out the new Kids registration form ahead of time online.

At the top of this page are links to sign up for the Resurrection Kids newsletter and to complete the new Kids registration.

Develop an About Us or Our Story page.

For many guests, both in person and online, a page where they can learn about what you believe, what your vision is for the future, and a little of the history of the church is important in their decision whether or not to worship with you. They want to know if what you believe is in alignment with their deeply held values, and whether they will be comfortable at your church. *Make your About Us page as much inspiration as it is information, so that people not only get the facts, they also feel a desire to belong, to join in the work your church is doing in the world.*

Provide a method for people to ask questions.

Sometimes people just won't be able to find what they're looking for on your website, or they might have a specific question to ask. Provide instructions for calling the church or include a link for them to submit their question by email (and then make sure the response is prompt). Prompt doesn't mean instantaneous, but inquiries from the website or phone messages should be returned by the end of the next business day.

Social Media

A social media presence that is also warm and engaging will reinforce and boost your church's image in your community. One caveat though: if you're going to be on social media, keep your profile fresh with regular postings.

A guest will likely first encounter your social media presence by seeing a post that one of their friends has shared on their personal social media. For that reason, social media can be an unofficial representative of your church—a recommendation, a conversation. Be authentic and less formal on social media. Let your fun side (and your quirks) show. Did the children at Vacation Bible Camp have a shaving cream fight? Did the youth choir sing in service last weekend? Last fall, our hometown Kansas City Chiefs were playing the Green Bay Packers, and we encouraged our community to wear their Chiefs gear to church. We posted a picture on Facebook with our pastor standing between one man with a Chiefs jersey and another with a Packers jersey, captioned "We truly do welcome all!" An openness to show your lighter side helps people who interact with your social media see you as a group of people instead of an institution (especially if someone who participated in the event shares it on their personal social media). Encourage your leaders to share the church's social media posts on their own accounts to increase your reach.

Mix up the types of messages on your social media. Celebrate moments, recognize volunteers, promote events, ask questions that encourage a response. Include photos or videos often, as these posts get more likes, shares, and comments than all-text posts. More activity = more visibility.

I described one Facebook post above. We post short video clips from the past weekend's message, or pictures of our Trunk or Treat event. We also post promotions for upcoming events or sermon series that we encourage our congregants to share on their personal social media as a means of inviting someone to church. Our pastors frequently ask followers on their personal social media to respond to questions that might shape their sermons or provide a sermon illustration for an upcoming weekend.

If someone comments on your social media post, respond. Even if you just say thank you, a response cultivates the relationship. It opens the pathway to conversation. If a person posts a negative comment, respond with as much grace as possible, and perhaps even apologize if their point is on target. If someone posts an inflammatory comment, you have a few options. You can ignore it (what we've noticed is that usually other people who see the post will make your argument for you), you can respond (we don't recommend this, as it usually leads to a downward spiral), or you can delete it.

Here are a few other tips about boosting your online presence:

You can merge your Facebook Page and Place, so that your church shows up in both sections when a search is done with the name of your church or even part of your name.

Claiming your profile on Google is a free and easy-to-use service that allows you to take ownership of your "business" profile on the search engine. Don't get caught up in the business terminology. Think of it as claiming your organization. Claiming your profile on Google enables you to manage your online presence across Google, including search and maps. When a search is done for churches in your area, your church will show up in a listing, with links to your phone number and website. Google My Business allows people to post reviews of your organization and enables you to respond.

It also gives you access to insights about how many searches are done related to your church and where the searches are originating from (close to you? within ten miles?) When you enter "churches near me" and a box pops up with a list of churches—those are churches who have "claimed their profile" on Google. All others fall below the box. Many churches have not yet claimed their profile on Google, and they're missing a prime opportunity to increase their visibility in their community and make it easy for guests to find them. Another important thing to note about this: if you don't claim your profile, Google fills in hours, website, and photos that they think apply to your church, but it's often wrong. Claiming the profile lets you edit the information and ensure it's accurate.

If you have the capacity to live-stream or post a pre-recorded video of your worship services, you greatly expand your reach. Making online worship available has allowed us to reach people in assisted living centers who can no longer physically make it to a church location, as well as parishioners who travel or are experiencing illness. It is increasingly becoming how people first experience church.

Carey Nieuwhof, author, podcaster, and founder of Connexus Church in Ontario, Canada, said this about online worship services: "Church online will become a front door for the curious, the skeptic and the interested. It will be the first stop for almost everyone, and a temporary resting place for people who are a little too afraid to jump in until they muster the courage to jump in through physical attendance."[2]

Since COVID-19, we've seen a significant number of people choosing to worship online permanently, and for them, your digital front door may be the only door they ever see. Make sure it's guest friendly and welcoming.

The digital world of websites and social media isn't just for businesses and individuals anymore. Today the internet is the first place we look for any information. Your website and social media outlets are your digital front door. Most guests will check your church out online before they visit you in person or attend an online worship service. Their first impression begins there; make sure it's a great first impression. Your online presence should build anticipation for the warm welcome guests will receive from your church community.

CHAPTER CHALLENGE

1. Review your existing website. Does it "feel" warm and welcoming? Does it make finding the information guests need most easy to find (location, worship service times, what to expect)? What one change could you make that would generate the biggest improvement?

2. Consider whether it might be feasible to create a single page on your website where guests and members can find the timeliest information about events and activities. What kinds of events could you feature that would be inviting for new people?

3. Brainstorm (with a group) ideas for types of posts you can make on social media that will include photos or video and invite participation from people outside your church. Create a shared file for photographs and encourage staff and key volunteer leaders to get into the habit of taking photos and saving them to that location, so they're easy to find when you're looking for a photo to use on social media.

5

PROVIDING AN EXCELLENT IN-PERSON EXPERIENCE

YVONNE GENTILE

Excellent hospitality helps us ensure a great guest experience—one that people will talk about to their friends. Keep in mind that a first-time guest will typically share their experience with friends, neighbors, and coworkers between eight and fifteen times (more if it's a bad experience). If we provide a poor experience on the front-end as guests arrive, the impression they form of our church may be difficult for excellent music and preaching to overcome. But an excellent guest experience, one with radical hospitality, creates an opening for the Holy Spirit to work.

An image of Jesus in stained glass, arms outstretched wide, greets all who enter our sanctuary at Resurrection's Leawood location. It's a picture of the welcome and love of Christ for all people—rich and poor, healthy and sick, those doing well and those enduring tough times. It reminds me that God welcomed me first, which makes me long to offer that same welcome to others, just as Paul describes in Romans: "So welcome each other, in the same way that Christ also welcomed you, for God's glory" (15:7).

One summer while on vacation in Colorado, I rolled my foot and broke a bone along the outside of the foot. I saw a doctor who put me in a boot and instructed me to use a knee scooter for eight weeks. The scooter made getting around so much easier, but it was dangerous if I was moving too fast and hit a small stone or a groove in the sidewalk. My husband and I had tickets to see a concert at an arena in downtown Kansas City about halfway through my time in the boot, and I was nervous about navigating the sidewalks and streets of the city, not to mention the crowds in the arena. I began to worry that we might need to pass on the concert, but I remembered from a previous visit to this arena seeing a person wearing a shirt that said "GUEST SERVICES" on the back, and decided to call their Guest Services department to see if they had any suggestions or capacity to assist me.

The Guest Services manager who answered the phone told me, "Please don't have any worries about this at all. We are well-prepared to assist you and will make sure you have a great experience. If you arrive before 5 p.m., there's a parking lot adjacent to our building that will minimize the distance you have to travel on your scooter. As you approach the building, we'll be looking for you."

I believed the part about the adjacent parking lot, but I was skeptical that anyone would be "looking for" me. However, I was willing to give it a go (I really wanted to see this concert!). We arrived about 5:10 and parked in the adjacent parking lot with no problem. Since the concert didn't start until 7 p.m., we made our way across the street (which is closed to traffic on event nights) to have dinner. Around 6:15, we started toward the arena.

Much to my surprise, when I rolled onto the sidewalk in front of the arena, I noticed a young man standing at a door waving me toward him rather than toward the lines of other attendees going through metal detectors and entering the arena. My husband and I went to his door, and he greeted us, "Good evening! I'm so glad you're here. I noticed your scooter and want to help you get through the crowd to your seats. We'll do a quick scan of your scooter and bag here, and then you'll head right to that woman" (pointing to a woman waving at us from another door), "and she'll help you from there."

The next woman looked at our tickets and escorted us to an elevator. The elevator operator made conversation with us as we went down to the floor, where another woman met us at the elevator door.

She told us, "Hi, my name is Sandy. I'm going to help you find your seats, and then I'll take your scooter and park it in this little pen over here so it's not in the way of other guests as they arrive." She put a tag on the scooter with my name, cell phone number, and seat number on it, and showed us to our seats. As she turned to take my scooter back to the pen, she said, "If you need to use the restroom or get a soda, or need to get up for any reason, just flag down an usher and they'll bring your scooter to you." I was impressed, to say the least.

Over the next ten minutes, I noticed the Guest Services team members helping a man with crutches and another woman with a wheelchair with the same service they provided me. The usher did indeed bring my scooter to me when I needed to go to the restroom, and then pointed me toward a restroom that would have a shorter line. I thanked him and told him as someone who works in the guest services field, I was impressed by the quality of their service. He smiled broadly and responded, "Thanks for telling me that. I love what I do and feeling like I make a difference."

What really blew me away, though, was toward the end of the concert, when I felt someone tap me on the shoulder. It was Sandy, bringing my scooter back to me. She said, "There are four songs left after this one. If you want to make your way back to my door before the last song, you can listen to it there, and we can help you exit without fighting the crowds." She did the same thing for the other people I had noticed her serving.

And so that's what we did. At the next-to-last song, we went back to her entrance, listened to the last song, and she escorted us to the elevator, where the same elevator operator took us back to the street level. We were out of the arena and in our car in five minutes, no jostling, no backup, no crowd. I was moved to tears at how well they cared for me—at a concert!

I keep thinking about the man's response: "I love what I do and feeling like I make a difference," and I just can't help thinking that we, the church, are called to love and care for people in a way that makes a difference. We may not know the impact our hospitality has on people in the moment, but we hear stories of impact afterwards, or see the results as people return, grow in their faith, see their lives change, and begin to serve others.

An excellent in-person experience onsite doesn't happen without intentionality.

Think about how you prepare to host guests in your home (especially first-time guests). You clean and tidy your house and yard. If they're an important guest, you might even edge the driveway. You fluff the towels and purchase supplies they might need to make their stay comfortable and enjoyable. Finally, you turn the lights on to create a welcoming atmosphere, and stand at the door, ready with a warm greeting. The same is true in preparing for guests at church.

We sometimes forget what it feels like for a guest to walk through the doors of our church for the first time. They are feeling a little unsure, sensitive to judgment, or afraid of being pressured into something they're not ready for. If they have small children to get up and ready for church, they're also likely stressed out before they even leave their driveway. They come with needs, fears, hopes, and expectations.

Rich Birch, a pastor, author, and speaker who founded the *unSeminary* podcast, released an episode in 2018 that talked about five emotions a first-time guest might experience:

- **Fear:** They have an internal dialogue that makes them put their guard up. They wonder, *Will I be judged? What if I look out of place? What if I don't know what to do?*
- **Confusion:** If a guest has difficulty finding bathrooms, coffee, or where they take their kids, it can be a roadblock. It's disorienting not to know where to go.

- **Regret:** This emotion is a little like buyer's remorse. Guests may think, *I feel so awkward. Why did I come? Where's the closest exit?* Their instinct is to turn around and walk out.
- **Hope:** This is the driving force that brings guests to church. Every guest who comes is looking for hope about something, and we are a people who believe the worst thing is never the last thing. We radiate hope (or we should).
- **Distraction:** This is everything else happening in their lives, and every distraction they encounter at church. Our goal is to remove distractions, help them transition, make sure they can understand and follow what's happening.[1]

If we prepare for guests well, we calm their fear, erase their confusion, prevent their regret, remove distractions, and help them find hope. Andy Stanley said it best in his book *Deep and Wide*: "To capture the interest of unchurched people…we must remove every possible obstacle from the path of the disinterested, suspicious, here-against-my-will, would-rather-be-somewhere-else, unchurched guests. The parking lot, hallways, auditorium, and stage must be obstacle-free zones."[2]

As we discussed in the previous chapter, guests form an impression of your church when they encounter your online presence. When they visit, a guest's impression of their experience at your church begins when they turn onto your property, and then it's shaped and formed by everything they see, hear, smell, and experience. Your physical space and in-person experience either confirm the great impression they formed online or begin to erode it. Paying attention to the details is critical, as each one is a touchpoint that impacts a guest's experience.

Let's explore some of the details that impact your guests' onsite experience, including outdoor signage, the parking lot, the physical space, indoor signage, your children's ministry, personal interactions, and the worship/event experience itself.

Outdoor Signage

Do you have clear outdoor signage? Can people find their way onto your property and to your building? As much as possible, you want to have clear, easily readable signage to help people navigate your location. Signs with white lettering on a dark background are easiest to read. Keep your signs simple—as few words as possible in as large a font as possible.

Sometimes this isn't as easy as it sounds. At some of our locations, we have multiple entrances and exits, and the parking lots can be kind of confusing. At our Leawood location, we're limited by the city's tight restrictions on outdoor signs, and currently the only permanent outdoor sign at the street is on the east side of our location, although our sanctuary is on the west side of our property.

We created temporary signs to help guests navigate to our building until we can get a more permanent sign approved. We also purchased sandwich signs and tall flutter flags to help guests identify our primary entrance and to provide a welcoming message that sets the tone for the guest experience inside. These signs point guests to our guest parking section or have messages like "So Glad You're Here!" or "Free Coffee, Bright Smiles, Warm Welcome Ahead." The reverse side that people see as they exit carries messages such as "See You Next Time!" or "Thanks for Coming."

Using these signs was a learning experience. They work great at every location except one. At our Leawood location, we have a wind tunnel on the west side, where most of our people park for our sanctuary services. The wind is so strong on that side it will blow a weighted sandwich sign across our Leawood location and lay the flutter flags flat on the sidewalk, even with sixty pounds of weight on the base, so at that location we replaced the tall flutter flags with 4-foot-tall decals that say WELCOME over our primary entrance. We've also changed some of our sandwich signs to real estate signs at the windiest corner, which has helped a lot. Always be ready to reevaluate and adapt.

Parking Lot

You may have heard the saying, "The sermon starts in the parking lot." It's true. Your guests' decision whether to return is influenced by their experience in your parking lot. Friendly people who smile or greet them on their way in or a volunteer team who is responsible for providing a welcome as guests arrive can significantly improve a guest's impression of your church.

We strongly recommend clearly identified guest parking. Whether guests park in that section or not, when they see that you've designated parking spots for them, it communicates that you are expecting and ready for them. It demonstrates that guests matter to your church.

Reserved handicapped parking and handicap accessibility in your building are also essential.

We visited a church a few years ago because our next-door neighbor's son was being baptized there. It happened to be the church we had attended before we came to Resurrection. I wasn't looking forward to it, because I had visited this same church a couple of years earlier when a friend was guest-preaching. During that visit, no one spoke to me except my friend when I approached her after the service. As we got out of our car this time and started walking toward the building, we were greeted or welcomed by a few couples who were leaving the earlier service. They were simple greetings of "Good morning!" or "Good to see you today," but they made a positive impression. And a greeter held the door open for us and welcomed us in. It felt like a different church. Whether it was a new pastor or a passionate volunteer, someone had instilled a value of hospitality there.

Develop a parking team that both manages traffic flow and provides a warm greeting as people walk toward your building. There are certain times when we need to actively park people when they arrive, namely Christmas and Easter. Most of the time, though, we have plenty of parking for people. We want our parking team focused on safety, helping people find closer parking spots, but primarily, we want them to provide a warm welcome to our guests, whatever the weather is. Even if traffic flow isn't a problem at your church, having a parking team there to welcome people communicates to guests that you value their presence.

If guests receive four authentic smiles in welcome during their visit, they are likely to report having a great experience. The parking team is the first personal smile your guests receive at your church. Theirs can be a tough job—cold and snowy, steady rain, or blistering heat. Remind them to have fun and smile. If you have a grumpy parking team, they're not likely to leave a great first impression on your guests.

Know your weak spots and take steps to overcome them. Our West location had only one entrance/exit, and between their morning worship services the parking lot would be tied up in absolute gridlock. The focus of one capital campaign was expanding their parking and adding more exits to improve the experience in their parking lot. It's made a huge difference.

Physical Space

Sometimes we are so familiar with our surroundings that we don't notice little messes. The appearance of your property matters—a lot. We're not talking about how fancy your building is; this is about its maintenance and upkeep. Is the landscaping in good order? Is the building itself clean and well-maintained?

Here are a few examples from home: that pile of stuff that somehow ends up on my kitchen counter each week, mostly because "I'll deal with that later." Or the vine that seems to have completely swamped my forsythia bush in the back yard. Or the little patch of paint that now doesn't match where we had to replace not only the air conditioner last summer but our thermostat too—and of course it's not the same size as our old one. Every time I walk by them, I make a mental note to deal with them, but never really get around to it. But when a guest is coming over, they pulse like blinking neon lights, demanding immediate attention.

At church we might have signs on the door in January still advertising our Christmas program, or supplies left on a table that a ministry used for an event the night before but missed putting away. There might be a potted plant at our entrance that's wilting and turning brown, or overflowing trash cans between worship services.

These things aren't the event itself, they aren't the worship experience itself, but they are distractions that send a message to our guests. Our guests notice these physical distractions, and it gives a poor impression of our church. They signal to our guests a lack of care and attention, and make our guests wonder what else we're not paying attention to; they tell our guests we don't really think what we're doing is important.

Smell is important too. One Good Friday, as we were preparing our sanctuary for Easter services, one of our team caught a whiff of a foul odor. We checked the space, including the bathrooms, but didn't see anything that could be causing it. Our facilities team checked all the drain traps, thinking one might be clogged, but that was not the case. Finally, we learned it was something to do with sewer gas and should dissipate eventually. By this time the smell was overpowering, and we were in a panic. We were horrified at the thought of having this smell during our Easter services. We bought solid air fresheners and hid them everywhere! Luckily, by the time for our services, the odor had vanished, and we were able to pull all the air fresheners too. Make sure your space smells clean and fresh.

Indoor Signage

Last year our Tech Arts team hosted a volunteer appreciation event at a local Dave & Buster's. We walked in knowing it was upstairs but couldn't see any way to actually get upstairs. We stood in the middle of the room (which was a bit of sensory overload with the flashing lights and clanging bells) and began to turn in circles, trying to find a staircase or an elevator. We eventually spotted the elevator and headed that direction. The team was expecting about sixty people between the volunteers and their friends or family. The team leader knew he didn't want his volunteers—his guests—to experience that confusion, so he placed himself at the front door to guide people to the party spot.

When your guests arrive inside your space, is there indoor navigational signage to help them with wayfinding? This is an area where we have much room for improvement. Sometimes our signage is so subtle we need signs to support the signage (no joke), but we're working on that. Ideally your interior space is visitor friendly. Look at your space through the eyes of a first-time guest. Will someone walking in know immediately how to find the sanctuary? the nursery? the Sunday school classrooms or fellowship hall? What signage could be added or improved to help first-time visitors find their way?

Is there a clearly marked location for guests to ask questions, and is there a volunteer there for them to have a personal interaction with? We call ours the Connection Point, but yours may be the Welcome Desk or Info Station. Make sure you don't have an empty desk with print materials but no person staffing the desk. If a guest needs assistance or information, you want to have your best volunteers standing ready to provide personal attention.

A couple of years ago we realized we were drowning in print materials at our Connection Points. Every ministry had flyers for all their programming, and they often used insider language and weren't up to date. We decided all our brochures on our information rack at our Connection Point should be geared toward guests. For example, the front of the children's ministry print piece is labeled Children's Ministry instead of saying KiDSCOR, which a guest might not know. Our student ministry's piece is labeled Student Ministry instead of Rezlife. On the back there is a broad overview about the ministry that points them to the website for more specific information. This created some grumbling in our ministries, but our purpose of reaching nonreligious and nominally religious people was our filter in the decision. Our members know where to go or who to ask for information.

Coffee!

Set aside an area for coffee and refreshment stations. It creates a sense of welcome and provides social comfort. People feel more relaxed with something in their hand, and it creates an opportunity for social interaction. Encourage your regulars to pour a cup of coffee for the person next to them and engage in conversation. Since the first of the year, I have visited my eye doctor, my dentist, and had an oil change. At each of these places, I was offered a cup of coffee while I waited. If Jiffy Lube can offer coffee, so can we.

Children's Space and Programming

Take care that your nursery and children's areas are clearly marked and that there's a welcome team in place to smooth the transition for a first-time family. The space should be bright and cheerful, not to mention clean and fresh smelling. The programming needs to include activities that engage kids and help them have fun while they learn about Jesus. A system of check-in and check-out and security processes to keep children safe are critical. The biggest worry every parent has when they drop their children off is whether they will be safe.

Nothing gets a first-time family back to church more effectively than a child who leaves saying, "Wow! That was fun!" We recently got a response to a first-time guest follow-up, in which the guest said her son had not stopped talking about his Sunday school class all day and couldn't wait to come back. That's the kind of endorsement we all want.

Keeping in mind that most guests check you out online before they visit, do everything you can to alleviate their fears ahead of time by providing lots of information on your website about your children's ministry, with plenty of photos. If possible, create a video about your children's ministry with multiple views of your ministry and programming, and testimonials from kids and other parents.

Again, if a form needs to be completed before parents can drop their kids off, give them the ability to fill that out ahead of time. We have some new families fill out the form online each week, but it's more common for them to come new on Sundays and we have them register at each entrance. Even so, providing the form online helps the families know what to expect about our registration and check-in procedures.

Once they complete the registration form, our Resurrection Kids' new family greeters escort the family to the classrooms and introduce them to the class leader. Children who are new receive a sticker that lets teachers and volunteers know they are a first-time guest so we can be sure they have extra help and guidance from our volunteers since it is their first time in the classroom. We also provide a small gift to the child after their visit and send a note to the parents welcoming their child to our programming.

The Worship/Event Experience

For most guests, the first point of entry is worship, but keep in mind: **Guests form impressions of every ministry, every event they participate in, not just worship. Impressions lead to opinions, and opinions result in actions: rave reviews or criticism, returning or never visiting again.**

Put your friendliest people at your doors to greet guests warmly at worship and at other events you hold at your church. Theirs is the second smile a guest will receive (after the parking team). Providing a warm personal welcome as guests arrive is so important. Train your greeters to open the doors for guests as they arrive. Vary the mode and message of the greeting so they don't sound like records on repeat. Ron and B. J. are two greeters who serve at our 9:00 service, and they are great at this. They are gentle and offer extra assistance to the elderly, and whoop and high-five with young children.

Teach your greeters the basics of reading body language. When someone doesn't make eye contact, a wave and a friendly hello might be the best greeting. Other people will see your greeters and their whole face will light up at the sight of a greeter's smile. We want to greet without overwhelming people.

The Worship Space

Inside the worship space we have an opportunity to provide a third smile. We constantly remind our ushers that their job is primarily hospitality, to smile when they hand out bulletins and offer activity books and crayons to families with young children. They're also on the front line for noticing people in need, or issues like spills and messes. We begin each service with a pre-worship huddle, closing in prayer, asking God to work through our ushers to extend the love of Christ to everyone they meet.

Paying attention to detail in your worship space is essential. You want a clean and distraction-free environment. Some of our locations have windows that allow natural light into the space, which is great, except when the angle is just perfect for the sun to stream in and blind people in the seats. We use shades to filter or block the light at those times so our guests are comfortable (and don't have to wear sunglasses in service!). After the service, our ushers walk through each row, picking up any trash and cleaning up any spills, so the space is clean and ready for the guests in the next service.

If your church uses bulletins or programs for worship, make sure they are guest-friendly. Eliminate any insider language, and make sure you provide information a guest will want or need. When we returned to in-person services during the pandemic, we made the decision not to bring back paper bulletins. Instead, we point people toward cor.org /next, where they can find information about upcoming events /activities. One benefit of bulletins is that they give your ushers a reason to greet and engage with people as they enter the worship space.

Your Attendees

It's critical that we cast vision for our regulars to extend a welcome. We need to encourage them to go outside their comfort zone to make others welcome. At our membership event, our senior pastor tells people who are joining that their visitor privileges are being revoked; they are deputized to make other people feel welcome. We ask members to park farther away from the building. We ask them to move into the center of the row in worship, leaving the aisles for guests so they don't have to climb over knees and feet to find a seat.

We need to frequently remind our members that they also play a role in demonstrating radical hospitality. Vision leaks. Our people need to be reminded on a regular basis that they have an impact on a guest's decision whether to return. When we ask people at our membership event why they decided to make Resurrection their home, they often say they first came because they heard our senior pastor was a great preacher, but they came back again and again because of how our congregation made them feel.

The Worship Service

The worship experience itself needs that same attention to detail. We spend a lot of time planning each worship service down to the last element. Every worship element is timed, and we think through all the transitions. During the week we check all the graphics that are going on screens. We plan who'll stand where and how the next person on the chancel gets to their spot. In the minutes before we open the doors for worship, each speaker/musician does a sound check and practices their transitions.

We practice every detail not to deliver a perfect performance but to eliminate awkward silences and messy transitions, to remove every distraction so we can create a holy moment, an experience where people can connect deeply with the living God.

High energy opening music creates excitement in the room. The opening welcome from the platform is the fourth smile for your guests. The worship leader needs to make eye contact, smile, and invite people to actively participate.

Think about what guests need to know so they can follow what's going on. Last year we visited a church in another state. We didn't know who the leaders speaking from the platform were. It seemed that the congregants were responding to secret signals. When the pastor scratched her ear, people would bow for prayer. When the music minister adjusted his tie, they all stood and turned to the right page in the hymnal to sing. We felt lost, and we're church people!

Everyone who speaks during worship should introduce themselves or have their name in graphics on a screen. Guests have no idea who's who at your church. Provide some context for what they're going to experience in worship. Recap the sermon from last week if it's related to this week's sermon, so a guest can follow the thread. Give verbal instructions for every element that happens in worship, so guests understand what's happening and why, which will make them more comfortable.

Put the words on screens for every spoken or sung worship element. If your church doesn't use screens, make sure the words are in your program or bulletin. We assume everybody knows the words to the Lord's Prayer or our favorite worship song, but in reality, they don't.

Beware of church lingo and acronyms. Instead use language that everyone can understand. If you use an insider term, explain what that is. For instance, we might announce that Crossroads is having a cookout next Friday night. Do you know who that is? But if we say Crossroads, our ministry for people aged fifty and up, is having a cookout, we make things clear to people who might not be familiar with our internal terminology.

We still have a time in the worship service for everyone to stand and greet their neighbors. It's awkward, we know. But there's a good reason for doing it. Despite all our layers of hospitality, sometimes guests make it into worship without a personal greeting. Our greatest fear is that someone will come here for the first time and feel like no one noticed them—like they were invisible. We know some people come to church and hope to be anonymous. We'll let them remain anonymous if they want, but we don't want anyone to feel invisible.

We need to have an intentional welcome to guests in the worship service. Our pastors offer a special welcome to first-time guests when they invite people to register their attendance. You may use connect cards or attendance notebooks that act as your cue. Whatever the mechanism, it's crucial to have a process for gathering guests' contact information so you can follow up from any worship service or event.

A sermon that connects with the unchurched, that speaks to their heads and their hearts, is vitally important. It doesn't matter if your church uses the lectionary, sermon series, or whatever the pastor comes up with each week. If guests hear a message that offers the hope and love of Jesus, speaks into their daily life, and nudges them to some action, it will likely connect with them. Make sure guests know they're invited to participate in any call to action and provide clear directions on where to go.

Finally, keep in mind that the benediction doesn't end the guest experience. Encourage members, staff, and volunteers to extend a warm goodbye following the service. At our downtown location, the band, pastors, staff, and leaders all move into the entryway of their building to greet and extend an invitation to return to all their guests. It's a meaningful experience for guests when those who were leading worship make themselves available for conversation.

Have your welcome or information desk staffed after the service ends in case guests have questions. If you have multiple services, make sure your space is straightened up and prepared for the next service, so those guests walk into a welcoming environment.

Remember, everything speaks. A guest's first impression starts long before worship or the event they've come to attend begins. It starts when they think about coming, when they turn onto our property, and is shaped by everything they see, hear, smell, and experience. A clean and well-maintained facility, a bright smile of welcome, and a helping hand when they need assistance could have a greater impact on the person's decision whether to return or not than the sermon they'll hear.

In the next chapter we'll discuss creating an excellent online experience.

CHAPTER CHALLENGE

1. Think about a time when you were the newcomer or guest in an unfamiliar setting. Did you feel welcomed and involved, or out of place and uncomfortable? What experiences or interactions made you feel this way? How might you evaluate the guest experience at your church through this lens?

2. Evaluate your exterior and interior signage and property maintenance. Task your team with paying close attention to these things the next time they drive into your property and enter your building and to provide feedback on the experience. Is there signage that helps newcomers navigate your space easily? What areas of your space need a little attention? Work with your trustees or building committee to determine what needs to be cleaned up or fixed up, and take action on those items.

3. Ask someone to evaluate your worship experience. Does the opening song create energy? Do the leaders introduce themselves or have their names on the screen behind them? Do they provide context and instructions for each worship element? Do they use language free from acronyms or insider church lingo? Is there a specific welcome to first-time guests? Are the words to songs and prayers on screens or printed in bulletins?

4. What single change could you make to your worship experience that would have the biggest impact toward making guests feel comfortable and welcome when they visit?

6

CREATING AN EXCELLENT ONLINE EXPERIENCE

YVONNE GENTILE

Many churches began live streaming their worship services to online attendees well before the COVID-19 pandemic. Those who hadn't, had to figure out how to do it—and quickly. Suddenly in-person worship wasn't an option. Churches, businesses, schools, and restaurants closed their doors, re-opening weeks or months later as we learned more about the virus.

Resurrection had been live streaming our worship services for a decade when that happened, so we were more prepared than many, but it did cause us to evaluate how we felt about online worship and how we engaged with online audiences. Pre-COVID-19, online worship was something that a person did when they were sick or out-of-town—a last resort, and a poor substitute—as opposed to a valid way to worship any time. It was more of a "peer in and see what is happening in the sanctuary" experience. Let's be honest—we'd still prefer people to worship in person, but for the first time, we began to ask ourselves: "How can we intentionally move online worship from a passive experience ('watching' worship that's happening elsewhere) to a fully engaged experience?"

The first change for us was one that most churches also made. Rather than live streaming services (with a now empty room), we started pre-recording them, with the online audience in mind. We began with a welcome to everyone worshipping at home, with our worship leaders looking straight into the camera. During the welcome, we invited online worshippers to light a candle nearby, to symbolize the presence of Christ in their personal sacred worship space for the next hour. Our pastors preached directly into the cameras, which we moved closer to the platform so they could more easily make eye contact.

Early on in the pandemic, the bishop in our annual conference allowed us to celebrate Communion in online worship. We began inviting people to have bread or crackers and juice or water, whatever they had on hand, ready to serve themselves or each other Holy Communion.

In 2020, churches were experimenting with all kinds of things: parking lot church, Facebook Live, YouTube, drive-up Communion and drive-up Ash Wednesday services. The pace of innovation and change was hard to keep up with. Church leaders had to figure out so many things at once—what was possible, what was acceptable, and what was beneficial long term. As the old saying goes, "Necessity is the mother of invention."

Things have continued to change and evolve as we have all learned more about what our community needs, what our relative strengths are, and what we can sustain. One thing I'm sure about is that digital ministry and online worship are here to stay. People are already spending a significant amount of time online. Research shows that Americans spend almost seven hours daily connected to the internet.[1] YouTube is now the second most widely used search engine, right after Google (which owns YouTube).

Churches that are limiting their online presence in order to force people to come back to in-person worship are missing a great opportunity. People are already on the internet searching for and finding spiritual content online. Generation Z (people born between 1995-2009) and Generation Alpha (born between 2010-2024) are digital natives. They go to their phone or devices first. Barna's research found that 84 percent of Americans say they are spiritually open; 40 percent are more open than they were pre-pandemic. Here's the catch: they're open to all kinds of spirituality, not just Christianity. The question is this: when they search for answers on the internet, are they finding any results with a solid theological foundation or only the Gospel according to YouTube or TikTok?[2]

Knowing that digital ministry and online worship are not only here to stay, but they are also a growing trend, we need to figure out how to do them well. How do we create a sense of belonging, community, and active engagement online? What makes for an excellent online guest experience?

We know that the online worship experience is not the same as an in-person experience. In person it is easier to stay fully engaged in the service; you're more likely to sing along to worship songs, and there is a sense of community and belonging that's hard to replicate online. For some who have health or mobility limitations, or other schedule conflicts, worshipping online isn't an alternative, it's their only option. For others, it's become a preference or a habit. But just because the online experience isn't the same as in person, that doesn't mean it can't be engaging and meaningful.

Hospitality Matters Even More Online

It is very easy for online worshippers to be passive and anonymous. We, as leaders, have to be very intentional about creating an engaging experience that draws the online attendee in, that captures their attention. Here are a few key things to keep in mind (compare these to the tips for an excellent in-person experience and you'll see some differences, but many similarities):

- **Keep Your Audience in Mind:** If you want your online audience to engage, you need to prioritize them. This is much easier to do if you pre-record your service or online content, rather than live streaming it, so online folks aren't stuck watching something that's happening to other people in some other place. That way you don't have to divide your attention between the people in the room and the camera, which is hard for anyone to do well. You can shift your language to resonate and connect with those online who might be watching later.

- **Simplify Functionality:** Your online experience starts with your website or whatever platform you use. For most churches, your website is the user experience for your guests. Make sure it's easy to navigate and participate in. If your worship service is buried ten clicks deep on your website, it creates friction for the guest. Make sure it's visible and easy to get to.

- **Clear Digital Space:** Remove unnecessary distractions from the screen, if possible. Yes, you want to have links for various functions like giving, registering attendance, submitting a prayer request, but a view that is cluttered with text and other images will make it hard for the worshipper to focus.

- **Make Eye Contact:** Every leader on the platform should make eye contact with the camera during the service. This has become more comfortable to most of us thanks to Zoom calls and Teams meetings. A person in an online meeting who never makes eye contact with the camera seems disengaged. That doesn't mean staring into the camera every moment, but when speaking to the audience, it's essential.

- **Smile, Welcome, and Greeting:** A smile, a verbal greeting to those joining online, and a word of welcome are important tools to deliver hospitality at the beginning or early in the service. Having a regular online host who offers that first welcome and greeting can help people feel connected to a person.

- **Mind Your Language:** Think carefully about your language, any announcements, or other things that might be said that wouldn't be relevant to someone online. You'll want to avoid saying things like, "Thanks for joining us this morning" because they may be watching at night or even two weeks from now. Or "Right after the service the Women's Ministry will be selling cookies in the lobby," because the person worshipping online can't just stop by to pick up cookies. Those little elements can create a disconnect for the online worshipper. Again, this is easier to do if you pre-record your service separately for the online audience.

- **Make It Easy to Go Deeper:** As much as possible, make available online any resources or giveaways that you're offering your in-person guests. For instance, we've sometimes had small cards with Scripture verses available for in-person worshippers to pick up. We upload a PDF that online worshippers can download and print or save, so they can fully engage. Are you offering a class or study related to your message? Can you make that available for the online audience as well?

Encourage Engagement Over Passive Viewing

Set the tone and expectation for active participation by having your host welcome online worshippers and remind them that worship is something we do, not somewhere we go. Give them instructions for how they can participate. A few ideas are:

- Light a candle to symbolize God's presence with you during worship.
- Grab a Bible, and something to take notes with (plus any elements they might need during worship—a bowl of

water for remembering their baptism, bread or crackers
and juice or water for Communion).

- Ask participants to fully participate—to stand and sing
  along to the worship songs, to bow and pray when
  invited to do so, to register their attendance, and so on.
- If your platform offers a chat feature, encourage your
  online host to serve as moderator and to add comments
  and questions in the chat for people to respond to.

Be Strategic about Your Online Presence

As church leaders realized that the pandemic shutdown wasn't
going to be "over" in just a few weeks, there was a flurry of activity
to create online ministry offerings of all kinds. Some of those worked
really well, and some didn't, at least not for my home church.

Replicating our in-person programming (that is, for kids or
students) online had some engagement during the early days of the
pandemic, but that waned significantly, and once in-person programming returned, it just wasn't sustainable. And sustainability is an
important factor to consider when deciding what to offer online.

For some churches, pre-recording or live streaming every worship
service isn't feasible from either a personnel or financial resource
standpoint. But could you pre-record a 5-to-15-minute message on
your smartphone to post on your church's Facebook page or YouTube
Channel each week? Instead of worrying about being all things to all
people, think strategically about how you can use technology to reach
new people or try new things, rather than duplicating everything you
do in person.

We've moved away from duplicating in-person programming and
are focusing on making "milestone moments" available online as a way
to offer entry points to new people—confirmation, Third-grade Bible
Exploration, Men's and Women's Conferences, Special Teaching Events,
and even Serve Trips. These, for us, have the highest strategic priority
as they can move someone into a deeper relationship with God.

One thing that is working is online discipleship groups. Many small groups began meeting via Zoom during the pandemic. While some of our groups that met online during COVID-19 have now returned to meeting in person, others have continued to remain primarily online. I recently spoke to a few leaders who have now been leading online small groups for four years, and they shared their best practices for offering hospitality and building relationships with online groups:

- Start each year with a new group covenant and have everyone re-introduce themselves. Set basic ground rules for turning cameras on and participating in discussions.
- Reach out to each new person to welcome them and listen to their story. This helps the leader build a connection.
- Spend time each week reconnecting. Follow up on comments and joys and concerns made during the prior session. Post prayer requests in the chat.
- Record each online gathering and post the recording in the chat so those who have to miss a session can catch up later.
- Break into smaller groups for discussion time. Some people will never speak on screen with ten other people, but they will in a group of three or four.
- Follow up with people who miss sessions, so they know they were missed.

As you think about your digital ministry, it's important to identify what you can do well, and play to your strengths, but don't be afraid to try new things. Start somewhere and improve from there. Experiment, evaluate, learn, and revise. Remember that scale is relative, and comparison is counterproductive. Jon Acuff, author and speaker, said, "Never compare your beginning to someone else's middle."[3] What can your church support financially, and what is sustainable for you and your team? Who can you invite to help you? Are there high school or college students in your area who create online content for fun and who might be willing to help?

Find and Use Free or Inexpensive Tools

Digital ministry and online worship don't have to be expensive. In chapter 4, I listed some affordable website tools that don't require coding capabilities. A smartphone with a tripod, good lighting, and a microphone attachment is sufficient to record short video segments for social media. You can now buy all the equipment you need to create higher quality content for less than $1,000, and Facebook and YouTube are free.

I can't close this chapter without at least mentioning Artificial Intelligence (AI), a technology that's already ingrained in our daily lives. AI is what powers personalized recommendations on Amazon and operates devices like Google Dot or Amazon Echo through algorithms and coding. While aspects of AI can be unsettling, such as targeted ads based on supposedly private conversations, the emergence of generative AI, using large language models, is noteworthy. Large language models use normal, conversational language prompts to return results.

One well known large language model AI, ChatGPT, was released by Open AI in November of 2022, and evolved to Chat GPT-4 by March of 2023. Beyond Chat GPT, a growing variety of AI-powered software is available, including some tailored for church leaders. Experimenting with Google's AI software (originally called Bard, now Gemini) yielded quick results in generating blog posts. However, AI output requires review and editing. Kenny Jahng, editor-in-chief of ChurchTechToday .com, compares AI results to something you'd get from a first-year seminary student—capable but needing supervision. Precision in prompts (what you ask AI to do) enhances results, and loading more content into AI refines its ability to return results in your voice and style. Be aware though, that sharing content with AI relinquishes proprietary control.

AI tools present opportunities for church leaders, saving time and providing resources previously out of reach. Applications like Dall-E, MidJourney, and others convert verbal prompts into images, and services like Church.tech.com can generate study guides, sermon clips for social media, and transcripts from uploaded sermon videos.

What role does or will AI play in hospitality? Currently, many websites feature chatbots that are powered by AI, and provide answers to guests' questions or help with routine customer service issues. AI is evolving quickly, and I anticipate it will continue to be refined and improved and become more robust in its capabilities.

While exciting, challenges with AI exist, raising ethical concerns and questioning the authenticity of AI-generated content. Addressing these concerns is crucial, but ultimately, AI is a tool—its impact depends on how responsibly we utilize it.

Digital ministry and online worship are here to stay. They are part of an emerging model of church. For hundreds of years, the church's model was gathering in person every week. That was HOW we did church. Our mission is WHY we exist, and the church's mission hasn't changed. It is to share the good news, to create disciples, and to work alongside God to restore the world to its intended wholeness. And we should be willing to employ any effective model we can to accomplish that. As Andy Stanley put it in his book, *Deep & Wide*, "When a church fails to distinguish between its current model and the mission to which is had been called and mistakenly fossilizes around its model, that church sets itself up for decline."[4]

In the next chapter, we'll explore effective follow-up, which cannot be done without great intentionality. Excellent follow-up can help turn a guest into a regular and make a member feel loved—a part of a bigger community of belonging.

CHAPTER CHALLENGE

1. Watch one of your online worship services or other digital ministry offerings expressly to evaluate the guest experience. Is it guest friendly? Is it warm and welcoming? Does it encourage active engagement, or is it a passive experience? What improvements could you make?

2. How has your online ministry evolved since it first began? What are some things you could experiment with to reach new people online?

3. Conduct a strategic assessment of your online presence. Review your website and digital platforms to ensure they are user-friendly and easily navigable for both guests and regular attendees. Identify areas for improvement and implement changes to create a seamless and engaging online environment for your community.

4. Spend thirty minutes a day for one week experimenting with AI. Consider how it could potentially enhance your ministry or enable you to do things you can't do manually.

7

INTENTIONAL FOLLOW-UP

YVONNE GENTILE

What our guests experience in those first few minutes, before the worship service or the event they've come to attend starts, sets the stage for everything that follows. Many of them came seeking something—comfort, hope, connection. Others may have been dragged to church by a loved one. They're looking for excuses not to have a good experience. Radical hospitality ensures that whatever their reason for coming, they have a great experience.

But our goal as a church isn't just to give people a great guest experience. We want them to return, to grow in their faith. Our purpose at Resurrection is to build a Christian community where nonreligious and nominally religious people are becoming deeply committed Christians. About 50 percent of the people who come to our church for the first time either have no faith background or they haven't actively been practicing their faith for some time. They come seeking connection. They are curious, but also questioning, cynical, and perhaps even returning to church after a long absence due to a painful or hurtful experience at a church. Intentional follow-up with guests is a critical part of what we do, to encourage them as much as possible to come back.

Our guest follow-up is an extension of our hospitality and the guest experience, so the messaging and approach are critical. We need to communicate to guests that they already belong or make them feel they could belong. We increase the chances of connection with excellent follow-up.

Follow-up is incredibly important. I remember years ago interviewing for a job at a large retailer in another state. I thought the interview had gone well, but believed they'd eventually select an internal candidate. It was a segment of retail in which I didn't have experience, and the role was one I hadn't done before. I waited for the "regrets" phone call or email for weeks, then months. By the time it came (three full months later), I was angry and feeling disrespected. Rejected—for a job I never expected to get in the first place. The fact that they didn't bother to give me the courtesy of a timely response told me that I didn't matter to them at all.

Faith Perceptions, which does research related to the first-time guest experience in churches, published a blog post in 2016 related to guest follow-up. Between October 2015 and September 2016, they surveyed 1,341 people who visited churches for the first time, all sizes and denominations of churches. Of those first-time guests, 504 provided their contact info when they were asked to do so, but thirty days later, only 119 (24 percent) had received any kind of follow-up from the church they visited. Of the 504 people who completed the information card, 359 were unchurched or dechurched. The fact that no one followed up with these guests sends a clear message that they were not important to the church.[1]

Knowing how to do excellent guest follow-up can be a mystery. Sometimes, even with the best of intentions, our efforts don't quite have the intended effect. We've all experienced follow-up that was more of a turnoff than an encouragement to return, and we know we don't want that.

Last year I attended a conference and heard one speaker that I really enjoyed. I wanted to hear more from him and so I signed up for his weekly email. Within days I was being bombarded with communication from him, often every day, promoting his latest e-book or online class, ALWAYS IN ALL CAPS AND NEON COLORS SO I WOULD FEEL THE URGENCY TO SIGN UP NOW! It was irritating and I ended up unsubscribing to all his work. I'm probably missing some worthwhile content, but his follow-up was just too much.

Your first goal should be to simply get first-time guests to come back. The primary goal in following up with a first-time guest isn't to get her or him immediately connected into a group or serving, or to become a member after a first visit, although that sometimes happens. The odds of guests making a connection substantially increase, though, after a second or third visit. In order to facilitate those progressive connections, we have to be intentional about how we do it.

Effective follow-up leads to returning guests, who (hopefully) eventually become fully engaged in the life of the church. Consider that a typical growing church sees 20 percent of first-time guests become part of the church. At Resurrection we're experiencing between 20 and 25 percent of first-time guests ultimately joining the church. For most growing churches, close to 60 percent of people will become part of the church after their third visit.[2]

We've found that there are three key components of effective follow-up—and these principles are true whether you're following up after worship or programming participation. Effective follow-up is prompt, personal, and pleasant.

Prompt

In 2007, Bill Easum published an article titled "How to Grow a Small Church." In that article he stated that the promptness of guest follow-up had a significant impact on their return rate to church. The best thing you can do is follow up within twenty-four hours. Bill's research showed that if you follow up within twenty-four hours, your guests are 85 percent likely to return. That's powerful stuff. Reach out twenty-four to seventy-two hours after their visit, and the return rate falls to 60 percent. Wait more than seventy-two hours and the return rate drops to 15 percent.[3] Prompt follow-up is an indicator to our guests that they matter to us. In today's environment of fast information and instant gratification, slow follow-up implies that their visit was not incredibly exciting or important to us. Remember this: if you wait until Wednesday to follow up with guests in worship, you are losing 85 percent of them. If you're leading ministry programming that happens on Wednesday night, you need to follow up before Saturday and ideally before Thursday night. Following up within twenty-four hours must be a high priority for us.

Personal

Make a personal connection. Guests aren't seeking connection with your building; they hope to find community. A person-to-person interaction is most effective in engaging guests. In our children's ministry, when a new child is checked into our KiDSCOR programming, the person who checked the family in sends them a handwritten note the same day. After worship, one of our volunteers delivers a coffee mug and offers a warm welcome to guests after their first visit. Make written follow-up personal by using your guests' names instead of a generic greeting.

Pleasant

Make sure your follow-up is a pleasant experience for your guests. This should be a no-brainer but it's often not. Design your follow-up to make your guests feel welcome and comfortable; ensure it's not intrusive or unpleasant to your guests. Sometimes in our efforts to identify and acknowledge new guests, we can unintentionally make them feel very uncomfortable. Remember, most guests prefer to wait until they've visited a few times before they let anyone know they're visiting. Let them fly under the radar during their visit if they like, just make sure their guest experience and your follow-up lets them know that they were not invisible.

We need to recognize the courage it takes for someone to come to church for the first time and be sensitive, navigating that fine line between excellent follow-up and something that feels more like church stalking. Pay attention to the feedback that you get from people, both verbally and nonverbally.

Commit to making your follow-up processes as light and noninvasive as possible, while still being committed to intentional follow-up. Use plain language with a friendly, conversational tone. The tone and tenor of our follow-up can create a positive emotional response in our guests when it's done well. And that's important because guests return not because of what we do, but because of how we make them feel.

Good follow-up is prompt, personal, and pleasant. Keeping these three principles in mind, let's shift gears to creating effective follow-up processes.

Follow-Up Processes

First, establish a reliable method to identify who your guests are and how many times they've visited, if you don't have one already.

As we mentioned in chapter 3, there are various methods for capturing guest information. Some churches have a designated location for guests to come and interact with staff or volunteers and might even encourage them to do so by offering a gift if they stop by. Other churches use connect cards that they ask guests (and sometimes regulars) to complete during worship and turn in later so they can capture needed information.

We use an online process for attendance registration of both members and guests. It can be a challenge to capture guest information, especially if they have concerns about being subjected to pressure to make a commitment before they're ready. Many guests will visit multiple times before they sign in. Something we experienced during COVID-19 was that often the first indication we had that someone was engaging with us was when they gave financially to the church, without ever registering their attendance. However, we can't follow up if we don't have their contact info, so we need to keep trying and making it easy for guests to self-identify.

When you've collected a guest's contact information, you can reach out to them for follow-up. Determine what your milestones will be, and the goal for each contact. With what frequency and for what duration of time will you follow up with guests? What is your desired outcome for each contact? Will you reach out every time they visit until they become members, only their first three visits, or some other frequency? For how long a time span?

It's important to be intentional about what you hope to accomplish with each follow-up contact. What information do you want to provide? What invitation to action will you give them? And more importantly, what emotion do you hope to inspire?

There's a story in the book *The Power of Moments* that illustrates this point. Michael Palmer was a professor who was leading a class on course design for other college professors. The goal was to help them think in a new way about how to create their syllabus for the class they were teaching. Most professors were simply taking the book they were teaching from and dividing it into the number of weeks they had for class. It wasn't very creative, but it ensured they got through all the material. Palmer asked the college professors to think about it from a different point of view. He asked them to answer these questions: six months from the end of your class, what do you hope your students remember? What are your dreams for them related to your class? He wrote their responses on a white board and asked if their current method of developing syllabi would move their students toward the dreams and goals they had for them. The answer was a resounding no. This gave them a new perspective, and they began to develop their syllabi with their ultimate goal in mind.[4] We need to have that same intentionality when crafting our follow-up messages. What do we hope our guests will remember about and/or do as a result of the follow-up we initiated?

As you reach out to guests, vary your communication methods. Use as many channels as possible, because some methods will connect with one group but not another, and vice versa. Use every method available to you and think strategically about when to use which method. Using a variety of channels also makes your follow-up more engaging and less likely to feel overpowering.

At Resurrection, our follow-up milestones are a guest's first, third, and fifth visit to a worship service. We try to space our contacts strategically, following up enough to let guests know we've noticed them and welcome them, but far apart enough that we don't become an annoyance. We regularly reevaluate, because what worked five years ago may not be effective today. To give you an example of what works for us, and help you imagine what might work for you, here is a summary of our follow-up process at Resurrection, starting with first-time guests.

Our Follow-Up Process

First-Time Guest

Our first-time guests receive a brief text message, a coffee mug, and a letter from our senior pastor.

The first contact a guest receives from us (if they provide a phone number) is a text message. There are several text messaging services available. Within twenty-four hours of worshipping with us—often the same day—first-time guests receive a text with a simple personal message:

> Hi Tina and Mark! This is Jay from Resurrection. Thanks for visiting!
> Do you have any questions about the church I can answer?

We make it personal. The team members sending our texts and checking the responses include their own names in the message, which also helps to make sure their texts don't get blocked, and we address the guest by name.

We love this capability! We've found that about half of our first-time guests give us their phone number, and about half of those respond to the message we send. That's a 50 percent response rate—it's tremendous!

Many times, the response is a brief acknowledgment: "No questions. Thank you for making me feel welcome. Will visit again soon." Those don't require a response in return from us. But frequently we get a response to our text that creates an opening for deeper connection. We received one response that said:

> Hello Jay. Looking to connect to a church family. Just moved to KC alone and want to find community. Thanks for reaching out.

We were able to have further conversation, learned that this young man had just taken his first job out of college and got him connected to our Young Adults ministry.

Occasionally we get a response that shares a deeply felt need, like one we received early last spring. It said:

> Thank you so much for reaching out. I've just been diagnosed with stage 4 breast cancer and want very much to get my husband and 3 little boys connected to a support system before my illness progresses. Can you help?

We followed up with this family and are providing care, ongoing connection, and support. Texting allows us to make a prompt and easy personal connection with our new guests. When we have guests that respond with more serious questions, we ask permission to move the conversation to email or telephone. No other follow-up process that we've used has enabled us to create that level of personal connection so quickly. Because we're committed to light, noninvasive follow-up, we don't text guests a second time unless they respond to our first message.

We also deliver a coffee mug to our in-person first-time guests within three days of their visit. We invite our entire congregation to participate. This is meant to be a personal but light touch, hopefully delivered by someone who lives in the same neighborhood. We train our volunteers to take less than sixty seconds to drop the mug off, and not to enter the guest's home even if they're invited. If the guest isn't home, they leave the mug by the door or in front of the garage door with a handwritten note. Showing up at a guest's home might sound intrusive at first glance, but because it's brief and all happens at the door, it becomes instead a personal interaction and a pleasant surprise, creating a memorable moment. Sometimes guests send us notes back, thanking us for the coffee mug and the warm welcome it represented. Delivering a coffee mug also helps our congregants remember that gut-fluttering feeling of being a guest, which reminds them of the importance of offering a warm welcome.

We mail mugs to online first-time guests, with a note. We began this process during COVID-19 and started with a simple A/B test. For an eight-week period before we re-opened for in-person services, we randomly selected half of the first-time guests to mail mugs to, while the other half did not receive a mug. At the end of the test, we discovered that the people who had received the mug in the mail returned at twice the rate of those who didn't receive a mug.

People ask why we give a mug and not something else. Some churches deliver cookies or other goodies, or give away Redbox codes and popcorn, and those are great too. We chose mugs because people tend to keep them. And unlike cookies that are eaten and then are gone, a mug often sits on a guest's counter all week with our church logo reminding them to visit again. We've heard people say nobody needs another mug, and we get it. But for us, this has proven to be not only a way to connect personally with guests; it is also an inexpensive and effective form of marketing.

The goal is to give people something that will keep our church name in front of them long after their visit. They use it, they see our name repeatedly, and they remember and connect it to their experience at our church. Here's a statistic for you: *People keep branded gifts on average for seven months, and a third of people keep them two years.* That means our logo is quietly inviting them back to our church for a long time.

Finally, our first-time guests receive a welcome letter via email from our senior pastor the week of their first visit. The letter is always personalized with first names. It expresses appreciation for their visit and invites the guest to return the following weekend. You might be thinking, "that sounds like a lot of contacts." The reality is that most of our first-time guests won't receive all those contacts. Many first-time guests parse out the information they give us over several visits. If they only give us a phone number, they only receive a text. If they only shared an email address, they receive an email version of our first-time guest letter. Using a variety of contact methods helps us reach more of our first-time guests with at least one contact.

I mentioned earlier that sometimes we find out a person has been engaging with our church when they give a financial gift, but we have no record of them attending worship or other events. Our Donor Relations team sends a letter thanking them for their gift, and our location pastor sends a note about a week later, thanking them for engaging with us and inviting them to meet for coffee or tea.

Third-Time Guest

The next time we follow up with a guest happens when they attend three times within a twelve-week period. (As you can see, all of this is dependent on tracking attendance.) Each week we run a report of all guests who have met that threshold. Those names are then assigned to the care pastor at the location that they have most often attended. Our online third-time guests receive that email from our online connection and care pastor, who they will have seen serving as our online host. Some churches follow up with guests on their second visit—again, select the milestones that work for your church—and with a specific goal in mind. We selected their third visit because it signals to us that they have more than a passing interest in our church, and we use this contact to develop a personal connection to our pastors. Our pastors call or email the guests who've visited three times and invite them to come introduce themselves next weekend after service or to set up a time to meet for coffee. Our online guests are invited to connect via Zoom. Being contacted directly by a pastor makes a strong impact.

Fifth-Time Guest

The last follow-up step for us with guests is an invitation to our membership event, Coffee with the Pastor. In our process this happens when a guest has attended five times in one year. About two weeks prior to our membership event, we send anyone who's visited five times a folded notecard with a personal invitation to the event. If we don't have a physical address, but have an email address, they receive an invitation by email, and recently we've used text if we have a phone number for them.

Coffee with the Pastor is a two-hour event where they hear our senior pastor's personal testimony, learn more about what we believe, and learn our expectations of members.

At that point a guest has worked through all our follow-up processes. For most guests, that takes six months to a year. During that time, if they've connected into our other ministries, those teams are following up with them too. For example, if they joined us for a Serve Saturday event (one of our regular service opportunities at Resurrection), our missions team follows up with them to invite them to the next serving opportunity. Or if they joined us for a class, our discipleship team follows up with a good next step. Every ministry continually follows up to encourage progressively deeper engagement.

Each new member receives a small "welcome" gift following Coffee with the Pastor. It contains things like an Apostle's Creed magnet, a Resurrection shower tag, a Resurrection car decal, a pocket New Testament, and a copy of Pastor Adam's book *Why?* For our new online members, the gift box is mailed, and it also includes a candle in a votive with the image of the Resurrection stained-glass window, as a reminder to light that candle during worship.

Ultimately, we hope this follow-up leads to a deeper commitment level with the church so that guests feel such a connection that they want to make our church their home—to become part of our church family.

Membership

The goal of membership isn't simply to join an exclusive group though; it's to grow toward deeper levels of participation and involvement in God's work in the world. While many of our guests quickly get involved, that's not an expectation we hold of them. For members we have expectations of how they will get connected and involved in the life of the church.

Joining the church can be a pivotal time in a person's faith journey. At Resurrection we made the decision that we didn't want to make it difficult for someone to join, but we wanted to set a high bar for engagement once they do.

At Coffee with the Pastor, we explain the five expectations of membership, which align with the five essential practices of the Christian life, outlined in Pastor Adam's book *The Walk*:

1. **Worship:** every week, and pray five times a day (morning, meals, and bedtime).
2. **Study:** read the Scriptures on your own every day and with a group twice a month.
3. **Serve:** give your time and talents to serve others inside and outside the walls of the church at least once a month.
4. **Give:** in proportion to your income, with the tithe being the goal, and live a life of generosity toward others.
5. **Share:** let your actions and your words be a witness to your faith.[5]

Coffee with the Pastor is a great opportunity to cast vision for our value of Radical Hospitality at Resurrection to our newest members. Our senior pastor shares with our guests that, by becoming members, they are agreeing to have all their guest privileges rescinded. We ask them to begin parking farther away from the entrance when they come to church in order to leave the closer spots for guests. They are encouraged to sit in the middle of the row in worship, to leave the seats on the aisles for guests, to wear their nametags, and to register their attendance weekly.

We provide options for people to engage in the life of the church right after Coffee with the Pastor. We have significantly simplified our messaging to new members to create greater clarity, so people know what their next steps are.

We invite them to connect with a group for study and conversation, using our senior pastor's book, *The Walk: Five Essential Practices of the Christian Faith*, which reinforces our five membership expectations and sets a good foundation for growing in their faith.

We suggest Serve Saturday as a great opportunity to explore serving. Serve Saturday events are designed as easy, low-commitment ways for people to make a positive impact on our neighbors in the metro area, with options for serving both onsite and out in the community. Preregistration isn't required, so people can show up at 8:45 a.m., select the Serve opportunity they want to participate in, and they're done by 1 p.m. Online new members are encouraged to participate in churchwide efforts, but in their local community, by running a food drive in their neighborhood for food pantries in their area or serving at local nonprofit organizations.

We place stewardship commitment cards on the tables where people are seated at Coffee with the Pastor and ask participants to pray about making a commitment to give regularly to the church in order to support its mission and ministry. For those attending Coffee with the Pastor online, we provide a link to an online commitment card. We encourage them to start by giving an amount that feels doable to them, and then committing to increase that number each year until they reach a tithe. If they turn in a commitment card at Coffee with the Pastor, we give them a CEB Study Bible as a thank-you gift. It works—people stand in line to turn in their commitment cards! New members online don't have to stand in line to receive their study Bible—we mail it to them.

Participants are encouraged to share their faith in several ways. Three specific ways are to invite their unchurched friends to church, to read *Why?* and then pass it along to a friend who is struggling through a difficult time, and to be intentional about practicing five acts of kindness each week.

Member Follow-Up

Our members need follow-up too. Our data shows that if a new member doesn't connect to the church in some way during their first eighteen months of membership, they are less likely to stick long term. It can be easy for new members to feel that joining is the goal rather than the first step in their faith journey.

Each new member receives their location pastor's weekly newsletter, which contains information about upcoming ways they can get engaged. Online members get a newsletter especially for them, that uses very intentional language, such as "we are connected across the miles."

Once a person connects into a discipleship or serving opportunity, that ministry begins to facilitate progressive connections, inviting them into a deeper engagement with the intent of leading them to become more deeply committed Christians. Here's what we know: a person can attend worship every week without significantly growing in their faith. But serving or studying side-by-side with other Christians reinforces what we read in Scripture and what we hear in worship, and that leads to changed lives.

At the one-year anniversary of their joining, we send each member household a handwritten note card, expressing our congratulations and prayers for them, and inviting them to a specific event or activity that is coming up. Each time we send out these cards, which is about five times a year, we receive responses with requests from people looking to connect.

For some people, it's more about the timing of the communication and that the card in the mail hits them when they are ready to take the next step. For others, we believe it is the personal approach of a handwritten card with that team member's name and contact information that makes them feel more comfortable reaching out and asking for what they need.

Re-Connection

Because we also track member attendance in worship, we can follow up with members who are for some reason disconnecting with church. Every week we get a report of members who have missed four consecutive weeks of worship, and they get an email from their location team to let them know they are missed. We call this contact Re-Connection, and it's very light, with a goal of letting people know we've missed them, hope to see them in worship soon, and asking if there is a need we can provide assistance with. It is absolutely not a slap on the wrist for missing worship. We want them to know that we noticed they hadn't been there and they are missed.

Often we hear that the people we email have been traveling, or otherwise busy, but two or three times each month we learn of a person or family who is going through a crisis but hadn't even thought about contacting the church. We connect these people to our care team, and that makes a huge impact on folks—first of all, to even think that we noticed they were missing, and second, to provide much needed care they hadn't known was available.

The Re-Connection contact makes it possible for us to offer care for those who need care and celebrate with those who are rejoicing.

Once a person receives a Re-Connection contact, they have to attend worship (and register their attendance) again and then miss four more weeks before they would receive another Re-Connection contact.

Quarterly Lapsed Member Follow-Up

Another follow-up process we have for members is what we call our "lapsed member" contact. Each quarter, any member who has missed thirteen consecutive weeks of worship receives an email from their location pastor, again a light touch. The email simply says we've missed them and highlights exciting upcoming ministry events or classes. The letter serves two purposes: it helps us reengage people into worship, and (for the third quarter contact) it gives us an opportunity to reach out to them before our annual stewardship campaign begins, so the first contact they receive from us after Easter isn't asking for money.

Inactive Member Mailing

In January we send an email to all members who have not attended or made a financial contribution for twelve months. The email includes a link to an online form that allows them to provide updated contact info and to indicate whether they would like to remain a member or be removed from our rolls. This helps us maintain a pretty clean member roll.

All these follow-up processes are designed to help us connect (or reconnect) people into the life of our church, to show that we are attentive to the details, that we notice people and want to offer them personal attention. And that makes an impression on people.

I mentioned that I worked in the corporate retail environment before I joined the church staff. Part of my role involved traveling to our retail locations across the country. One of the things that amazed me was how often I'd meet one of our best salespeople—a million-dollar sales producer—in a small store that wasn't necessarily in the best location or didn't have the most up-to-date décor. I would ask them how they did it, and without exception, they all attributed it to the same practice: following up and developing a relationship with their clients. When they weren't actively serving a client, they were writing thank-you notes, emailing to tell them about special events that were coming up, or once a relationship had been established, calling to tell them about a new piece of merchandise that had come in that they thought the client would love.

Excellent follow-up is critical if we want our guests to return. Intentional follow-up signals to both our guests and our members that we care, that they matter to us. Saying you care from the chancel is important, but people will remember what you do (and how that makes them feel) more than they'll remember what you say. Let your actions demonstrate your desire to make every person—guest, member, wanderer—feel welcome and invited into your community.

Every time you make a guest feel welcome, you give them a taste of the kingdom of God. Every time you follow up with a guest, you invite them to participate in God's kingdom. If people are going to experience God's kingdom anywhere, it ought to be at and through the church.

CHAPTER CHALLENGE

1. Reflect on memorable follow-up experiences you've had, both good and not-so-great. What was the difference between a follow-up that made you likely to return to a business or organization and a follow-up that was more of a turnoff?

2. Does your church offer a gift to first-time guests? Is it consumable or something that will serve as a repeated reminder of your church's welcome? Brainstorm ways you can ask your members to fund the purchase of a tangible, lasting gift for first-time guests. For instance, at Resurrection, when we decided on mugs, we asked congregants to buy one for themselves at a slightly higher price than we paid for them in order to provide seed money for this ministry.

3. If you have online worship services, how are you following up with online guests? What can you do to make them feel connected and cared for?

4. Where do you see value in following up with both guests and members?

8

SAFETY AND SECURITY HOSPITALITY

DEBI NIXON

God has entrusted the care of his people into our hands. We recognize this responsibility to protect our congregants and create a safer church community. In Acts: 20:28a, we read these words, *Watch yourselves and the whole flock, in which the Holy Spirit has placed you as supervisors, to shepherd God's church.*

As the shepherds of God's church, we are called to protect our congregation, particularly children, students, and vulnerable adults, including those with special needs, mobility issues, hearing and sight impairments, and more. And we know the unexpected can happen at any time. The scope of what is needed to provide a safe space is broad. It requires plans for how to respond to medical emergencies, natural disasters, and unwanted intruders. It creates an expectation of safe spaces for minors and vulnerable adults. It requires a plan for how to respond to property crimes. And it demands protection of our congregants' financial gifts and data.

The art of hospitality comes with a responsibility for preparedness. This chapter focuses on how we create a culture that prioritizes creating safe spaces as a part of the hospitality ministry of our church. Not as an add-on, but as a foundational part of welcoming guests with exceptional hospitality.

As discussed in each previous chapter, the art of hospitality creates an environment where all feel welcomed. Creating this space of physical, emotional, social, and spiritual safety opens one up to experience God in greater ways. When one feels uncomfortable, unwelcomed, or unsafe, it is a barrier to experiencing all that God has in store for them.

People visit churches to experience peace, comfort, safety, and a sense of belonging. And most come believing the church is a safe place where they are protected. Nothing bad could happen at church, right? However, thinking or portraying the church as a place immune to safety and security threats is disingenuous. Violence at houses of worship in the U.S. is increasing. The most tragic and shocking incidents make the news and shock the public, yet many smaller incidents occur at churches weekly. Around 480 incidents of serious violence are estimated at places of worship in the U.S. each year.[1] These incidents range from those involving mental health disorders to family or personal disputes to theft—the motivation for the violence varies. This same study reported that 52 percent of the incidents occurred outside of the building, while 48 percent occurred inside.

We are often the first place those in need will come for comfort or support after experiencing a significant loss, medical diagnosis, relationship or other personal challenges. People approach churches when facing difficult economic circumstances. Some of these individuals may pose a threat as they have feelings of desperation or have mental health issues. Because of this commitment to serve all, thinking about safety and security on church properties can be complex. In addition to security incidents, medical emergencies, weather-related emergencies, and similar scenarios also requires us to have layered plans in place.

At Resurrection, we have had the unfortunate experience of vandalism, thefts, break-ins, protests, personal threats, tornado warnings, medical situations, and even a shooting in our parking lot. We don't make emergency and safety plans with the belief that "it won't happen here," but instead with the knowledge that "we must be prepared when it does." Preparation enhances your hospitality ministry by creating a safe environment, helps you actively respond in a crisis situation, and most importantly it saves lives.

The bad news is that natural disasters and medical emergencies can strike at any time and bad actors are out there. The good news is that your church does not have to sacrifice the experience of hospitality to create an environment that is more secure. A common fear is that making security and safety protocols more visible could make your church appear less welcoming. Yet when done well, the opposite will be experienced. Clearly communicated safety protocols let the congregation know you have taken the time to anticipate what is needed to ensure their safety. Instead of feeling fearful, they feel safer, welcomed, and loved knowing you have a plan. Safety and security plans should combine effective response to threats without changing the experience of hospitality for your guests.

So, where do we start?

Name Priorities

It's important to know first what you are protecting. Of course, first and foremost you are protecting people. You are also protecting church property, congregant financial gifts, your data and records, ministry and program continuity, and your reputation as a church. And you are protecting your staff as well. What other things would you include? Once you have identified all you are protecting, it is important to name the priority and vision you have for your facility safety and security ministry. At Resurrection our Safey and Security Team focuses on identifying and assessing risks impacting the church and determines responsive strategies that are documented for training purposes and monitored to prevent and prepare for an ever-changing threat environment.

Recruit Your Team

Look for those in your congregation who have experience in law enforcement, first responders, military or security backgrounds, doctors and nurses, education professionals, financial and online cybersecurity, insurance and risk management experience as examples of the diverse skills and expertise needed for your team.

The team should consist of those who are physically and emotionally qualified to collaborate on the development of plans, identify potential threats, be a constant learner, carry out their role not as an authoritarian, but with a spirit of hospitality, and would be calm and reassuring in responding in a time of crisis. From this team, select a security director or leader. Someone who has spiritual discernment and maturity, while also well-versed in overall safety and security protocols, risk assessment and management, and ability to train others.

Security team members should be fluent in protocols for the protection of minors and vulnerable adults, lockdowns, evacuation and response to disruptive guests, and medical emergencies. They should be familiar with the overall schedule of the church and programs, have awareness of service rundowns so they know who will be back of house, on the chancel, and so on. They should also know their specific assignments and roles. Schedule monthly team meetings to train and ensure proficiency with your plans and procedures.

Identify and Address Potential Hazards

Your team will want to start with a thorough assessment. There are so many different variables across churches that no resource is comprehensive for every environment. But an assessment will include looking for issues that impact safety, security, emergency preparedness, and the ability for your church to continue services and programs without significant interruption. COVID-19 is an example of a situation that challenged the continuity of services for many of our churches as we put social distancing practices in place. A basic assessment might include:

- Checking regularly for anything that might be a safety hazard or needs to be fixed.

- Conduct an audit of all the access points to the building and determine if you should limit access to a central location where all can be welcomed and greeted. Is each access point in working condition? Do doors and windows have secure locks?
- Is there ample lighting both inside the building and outside the building? Is backup lighting working in case power should go out? Are the timers working if outdoor lighting is set to come on at a certain time? Are exit signs clearly marked and lit?
- Is every person working with minors and vulnerable adults fully certificated and trained?
- Do you have an AED Defibrillator? If so, do you have trained volunteers? Have any medical supplies expired and need to be replaced?
- Have sprinklers and alarms had their annual testing?
- Is landscaping trimmed around the building to improve visibility and limit hiding places?
- Are donor's financial gifts and data secured?
- What security risk exists within your congregation? your community?
- Have volunteers walk the property and spaces during worship and various days and timing of programming simply to maintain awareness of what is happening. Train your leaders to look for hazards such as spills on the floor that might cause someone to slip, sidewalks that are uneven and need repair, areas that need to be cleaned of debris, suspicious packages or something that just seems out of place.

It is important that you address and take care of any problems you identify as promptly as possible. If a window is broken, a lock not working properly, security software is outdated, or the upkeep on the church not consistent, those with bad intents may see this and use it to their advantage. During one of our assessments, we realized that at several of our locations when the sanctuary doors are closed there is no visibility to the outside. At these locations, the doors have no side panels or view windows. To address this, we have volunteers assigned at these doors throughout the entire service.

Include Local Law Enforcement and Professionals

Invite your insurance broker, local law enforcement, first responders, and the Department of Homeland Security to be a part of your team. They have a mutual interest in keeping you safe. They will provide a risk assessment after walking through your building and property. One way to identify trouble spots and potential hazards is to have someone with experience point them out. Police officers, first responders, security experts, and fire marshals can help you better see the potential risks, offering ideas to create the safest environment possible.

These professionals can also share information and education on what is happening in the community, provide updated information on local and national risks, and work alongside you on strategies for keeping your facility and congregation secure. If we only keep our eyes on what has happened and create strategies around the past, we will miss that those with ill-intent spend their time thinking about how to do something unexpected. Kate Wood, who has championed Resurrection's safety and compliance policies and procedures says that "having a view of the horizon and considering what might rise to the level requiring response in your context allows you to be diligent and not complacent."

By developing a partnership with your local law enforcement and responders, it also ensures they are familiar with your building and property. The last thing you want is for emergency responders to be visiting your location for the first time in the midst of an incident. Let them use your building as a safe place to prepare reports, use the restroom, practice emergency rescue techniques, and more. For example, the police in our area use our parking lots for motorcycle training, and have used our buildings for intruder, hostage, and active shooter training. Find ways to make them a part of your community. Food might be a motivator, so invite them to church potlucks or surprise them with a breakfast or lunch. It's an act of hospitality to them.

You can also take advantage of free community trainings such as First Aid training, CPR/AED, or other seminars such as how to prepare for natural disasters or active shooter awareness.

Develop and Document Your Safety and Security Plans

Every congregation should have detailed plans. The plans should take into consideration aspects like potential medical emergencies, natural disasters, building hours, varying times of program usage including weekend worship when you likely have your largest number of people in the building at one time. It includes thinking through the impact of children's ministry, preschool programs, student ministry, small groups, recovery groups, church sponsored feeding programs, and more, and keeping all safe. It also looks at who has access to the building with their own keys or access badges, what hours do they have access, what outside groups use the building, data, cyber and money protection, and more.

What follows are ideas to help you get started on developing plans, processes, or policies to address improvement opportunities you've identified through your assessments.

Safety of Children and Vulnerable Adults

Safeguarding the physical, emotional, social, and spiritual well-being of children and vulnerable adults is our duty and responsibility. All children and vulnerable adults have the right to be safe and protected from harm in any and all environments—home, school, religious institutions, and in the community. The church must be committed to creating and maintaining an environment where all can worship, learn, and work together in an atmosphere that is safe. At Resurrection, we have developed a policy for the protection of children and vulnerable adults that states, we strongly oppose and prohibit emotional abuse, physical abuse, sexual abuse, sexual harassment, sexual misconduct, and other forms of exploitation or abuse of children and vulnerable adults. As churches we must acknowledge the unique position of trust the church, its pastors, staff, and volunteers hold in the lives of the people we serve. Protecting children and vulnerable adults must be the highest priority with an unwavering dedication to education, screening procedures, reporting expectations, independent and thorough investigations, and accountability.

We must be churches willing to do what it takes to meet all practices related to the care and safety of children and vulnerable adults. Not because we have to but because we are committed to demonstrating the love of Christ through our hospitality of safety.

Having a written policy documents the church's expectations regarding the prevention of abuse and practices pertaining to safe check in and check out. At Resurrection, while not exhaustively listed, these are some aspects of our policy:

- Minimum age for serving with protected people. At Resurrection, staff and volunteers must be at least five years older than the oldest child they serve. Any staff or volunteer under the age of 18 must be visually supervised by another certified adult.

- All serving must fill out a volunteer application, complete an interview by the ministry leader, consent to a background check (*parental consent is required to conduct a background check on anyone under the age of 18*), pass a certification process, and participate in abuse prevention awareness training.

- At Resurrection, we support the Two Adult Rule, meaning that at least two unrelated adults who are certified must be present in each classroom, vehicle, or enclosed space when online or in-person ministry involving protected people is taking place.

- Best practices include written guidelines establishing secure drop off and pick up to authorized individuals only, diapering and toileting procedures, allergy, medication, and illness awareness, photo and video capture, social media tagging, and more.

- Written guidelines on how to report suspected violations help to have good faith processes in place for proper investigation.

- Having a secure area that limits access and can be carefully monitored establishes boundaries for increased security and safety.

- Procedures for check in captures important information including allergies, medical and special needs, custody disputes, other siblings, and so on. And a check out process ensures children are only released to the proper adult(s). It is important to find a way to make this process easy, particularly with families with multiple children.

Procedures for Fire, Tornado, and Medical Emergencies

We know we cannot predict with much accuracy when a natural disaster might occur. Yearly, churches across the country are severely impacted by weather-related events such as tornados, hurricanes, floods, and fire. Church members experience medical emergencies while at church such as fainting, seizures, heart attacks, falls, and more. Having a plan on how to respond that directs each step saves lives. Aspects of your plan might include the following:

- Signage directing people on how to evacuate the building or where to shelter in place.
- Written instructions placed near or on the pulpit that can be easily accessed and read by whoever is leading. Having printed instructions and an easy-to-follow script allows the leader to respond with a sense of calm and assurance, guiding people to safety with a well-thought-out plan versus reacting in the moment to create a response.
- Well-stocked medical and trauma kits including an AED with trained volunteers who can administer care.
- Flashlights and backup lighting in the event power goes out, with reflective low vision tape guiding people to exits and identifying potential hazards such as steps.
- Emergency plans documented and regular training for lead ushers and volunteers on how to carry each out.

Responding to Intruders, Mental Health Intervention, or an Active Shooter

Yearly, children practice the unexpected at school by doing fire and tornado drills and active shooter and lockdown drills. This models the types of preparation we should be doing in the church. Your congregants assume and expect that we have a plan. They don't come expecting to feel unsafe while in worship, leaving their children in the nursery, volunteering, or attending a funeral.

Make it a priority to review each plan regularly and update as needed. Evaluation and modification are crucial for sustained effectiveness. By adopting a forward-thinking mindset, you are providing an environment that values maintaining safe, secure spaces for all to experience Christ.

Train Volunteers, Staff, and Congregation

With policies and procedures in place, it is imperative that you train your volunteers, staff, and congregation. You are likely aware of the adage, "rise to the occasion," but when it comes to the safety and security of your congregation, you don't want to rise to the occasion, you want to fall back on your training. It is difficult during a crisis to come up with the most effective response, so plan in advance, think about it in advance, practice it in advance so in the moment, you can trust your training to bring a good resolution.

A well-trained security team will be able to spot potential threats and respond accordingly. A team well-versed in the safety of minors and vulnerable adults will be better prepared to prevent unauthorized individuals access to children. Well-trained ushers, greeters, nursery volunteers, and parking lot volunteers give assurance more eyes are better when it comes to caring for your congregation and extending hospitality.

Your church will need to determine how visible you want security team members to be. Some churches keep their security undercover, while at Resurrection we value having our security team members more visible. We believe it sends a message to our congregation we have a plan in place for their safety, and it also dissuades bad actors. Visibility includes providing lead volunteers with headsets and two-way radios for communication, traffic safety vests, flashlights, access to fire extinguishers, and clearly marked greeter and usher badges. Volunteer emergency medical responders sit in easily identifiable reserved seats within the sanctuary with access to the AED nearby. Those certified for the protection of minors and vulnerable adults have clearly identifiable T-shirts or nametags. Staff as well as volunteer security team members wear a visible laminated lanyard and nametag. The key is to provide nametags and other identifiable markers that match the level of visibility you want for your volunteers.

At Resurrection, we have uniformed, off-duty law enforcement onsite in our public spaces like the lobby during worship and at most of our events. While this is likely not necessary for all churches, it is a choice we have made in response to our size and exposure in the community.

A fear you might name is that too much visibility could make the church appear less welcoming. There is merit to this if your team acts in ways that are intimidating, strict, rigid, suspicious, and perfunctory. The counter is to approach the role of protecting your congregants from a heart that is prepared and seeking to serve the body.

Ushers and greeters play an important role in your hospitality ministry of safety and security. These volunteers are typically the first to welcome visitors and create that first impression. Yet most have little experience in emergency planning or response, and likely signed up to serve as an usher or greeter thinking they would be smiling, shaking hands, serving coffee, opening doors, helping people find seats, and passing the offering plate. The good news is that is their primary task; however, they do share in the responsibility of ensuring the safety and security of your guests and congregation. Training for your ushers and greeters should include encouraging them to observe people and assess situations, helping them know where to find emergency information and instructions and letting them know who to contact should they need help. Any time an usher or greeter has a concern or is simply uncomfortable about something they have observed, it is important they don't try to address it themselves, but instead bring attention to it and seek help. All volunteers should feel empowered to "see something and say something," followed by having trained staff and lead volunteers with plans to "do something."

A great no-cost training solution is to use the Power of Hello[2] because it relies on our most significant resource, which is our people. The Power of Hello allows you to lead with hospitality. You can access resources and get more information at the Cybersecurity and Infrastructure Security Agency. The website provides a comprehensive guide to help secure your facility while sustaining an open and welcoming environment.[3]

You can have cameras, alert systems, and notifications, but the first persons to observe and activate those responses are people. This is where hospitality and safety and security so seamlessly connect. If you have people at your door(s) who are making contact with people and learning names, then every person who walks through the door feels seen. Not only is this an incredible practice of hospitality but it also dissuades those coming in to do harm, because now they have been seen and observed. So, if a bad actor was to come in, this act of hospitality would be a discouragement or barrier to dissuading them from taking any additional steps. They might notice cameras or signs later, notice security team members or uniformed officers later, but if they are seen, greeted, and recognized, it is a big hurdle for them to cross.

A Few Additional Tips to Being Proactive and Putting Safety First for All Who Come to Your Church

Assign Roles

In an emergency, it will likely be chaotic and confusing. It is important that your protocol clearly states who is in the decision-making seat. Everyone should be empowered to call 911, if necessary, but other decisions should be made following the established guidelines that not only document the action steps but name the person in charge. This includes assigning someone to be responsible as the key contact with the media.

Determine Methods of Communication

Determine in advance how you will communicate with one another. You can use two-way radios, headsets, or texting. What is important is to have a plan, particularly with those leading from the front of the sanctuary. It many cases it is the pastor, liturgists, musicians, and worship leaders who have the best view of the space. They are the ones who can span the entire room and likely have a better view of the doors to the sanctuary. It is important that you have a way to communicate with one another, including providing them with specific information on how to respond should an emergency arise.

Repeat, Repeat, Repeat

For those who travel on airplanes, you know before every flight, the crew makes safety announcements. It makes no difference if you are flying for the first time, or have flown a hundred times, the same message is repeated. You are familiarized with the aircraft, reminded of what to do in the case of an emergency, and encouraged to locate the emergency exits.

Pointing out exits at the beginning of a large service during a major holiday or gathering is a smart church security procedure. You can also point out where the ushers are sitting or directing them on who to talk to if they have questions or needs. You can say something like "if you have a medical or other emergency, here is who you go to."

Each year, plan a Security Sunday where you can do a quick reminder of all your emergency response plans. You can provide a document with a detailed map of how to exit the building, where to shelter in place, where first aid stations are located, and so on. By doing this you are sending a message to your guests that you have a plan, and you have prepared for them.

Churches that embrace creating safe, secure spaces view safety and security not as separate actions, but as a part of their hospitality ministry. They deploy not only the trained security team and staff, but everyone from parking lot volunteers to greeters to ushers to nursery workers, knowing it is better to have more eyes with awareness of the environment. You are not choosing between security and welcome. They are intertwined and it is a matter of finding the right balance.

Safety and security begin and end with the art of hospitality. You are worrying and preparing, so your congregants don't have too.

CHAPTER CHALLENGE:

1. **Name Your Priorities**
   - Identify and prioritize protection concerns, including people, property, financial gifts, data, and reputation.
   - Begin making a list of policies and procedures to create. While this list is not exhaustive, it provides a starting point for your team to focus on.
     ◊ Fire, weather, and medical emergencies response plans
     ◊ Safety guidelines for the protection of minors and vulnerable adults
     ◊ Limited access agreements
     ◊ Response to intruders, mental health intervention, or an active shooter
     ◊ Protocols for bomb threats
     ◊ Building hours, access, and monitoring
     ◊ Concealed carry policy for weapons on your property
     ◊ Financial, data, and cybersecurity guidelines
     ◊ Media relations and community response action steps

2. **Recruit Your Team**
   - Establish a Safety and Security Team focused on risk identification, strategy, formulation, and continuous monitoring.
   - Assemble a diverse team with backgrounds in law enforcement, first response, medical, education, and cybersecurity.

- Appoint someone to lead your Security Team with spiritual discernment, expertise in safety protocols, and the ability to lead and train.

3. **Identify and Address Potential Hazards**
   - Conduct regular assessments covering safety, security, emergency preparedness, and church continuity.
   - Address issues promptly, ensuring building visibility, lighting, access points, and landscaping are conducive to safety.

4. **Include Local Law Enforcement and Professionals**
   - Collaborate with local law enforcement, first responders, and insurance professionals for risk assessment and community partnerships.
   - Participate in free community trainings to enhance preparedness.

5. **Develop and Document Safety and Security Plans**
   - Formulate detailed plans covering medical emergencies, natural disasters, building access, program schedules, and more.
   - Specify policies for the safety of children and vulnerable adults, fire and tornado response, and intruder situations.

9

CREATING A CULTURE OF HOSPITALITY

YVONNE GENTILE

Most churches and organizations would describe their culture positively. Friendly. Focused on reaching new people. Making a difference in our community. Making church relevant. The challenge is that most of us shape our culture passively, if at all. We *want* to be these things. We think we are these things. But are we *really* these things? Do these words and phrases accurately describe our culture?

An organization's culture is the social behavior and norms found in its people. It's what they do every day. Unless we shape it with intentionality, we might find ourselves far off our desired course. If we want radical hospitality to permeate the culture of our churches, every staff member, key leader, and volunteer needs to be demonstrating it in their ministry setting. Our leaders have to show radical hospitality to our congregants, and our congregants have to practice it with one another.

In order for that to happen, we need to cast vision repeatedly, consistently for hospitality, keeping it front and center as a value of our church. If we recruit volunteers and train them to fulfill their role, but don't give them a vision that helps them see the impact their volunteer

117

role makes in God's kingdom, we're going to end up with volunteers who don't know their purpose. That eventually leads to volunteers who aren't committed, who may not buy into the culture we want, and who aren't great ambassadors for our ministry.

As the biblical proverb goes, "When there's no vision, the people get out of control" (Proverbs 29:18a). For this reason, in this chapter we're going to talk about casting vision and developing training first, then recruiting and onboarding, and finally, leading through change.

At Resurrection, we've been focused on radical hospitality since our beginning, yet the reality is that vision leaks. The natural tendency for every organization is to experience mission drift. We get distracted by one new project, then a major initiative and another, and pretty soon people are focused on the next item on their to-do list and they've forgotten the greater vision they're working toward.

In April of 2017, we opened our permanent sanctuary. Our Guest Connections, Tech Arts, and Facilities teams (and others) spent the entire year prior to that preparing to open the space: figuring out what we needed, ordering supplies, recruiting and training many additional volunteers. The scope of the preparations was overwhelming at times, and we had a hard deadline. For five months following that move, our focus was working out the kinks. If you've ever moved into a new space or implemented a new process, you know that you develop a plan, and then you have to adapt, because things rarely (never) work exactly as you had planned. It takes all your focus. That was our experience for more than a year as we moved toward opening our new space and worked out the details of the transition.

One day our team was sitting around a table, and someone made a comment about our team's purpose being to make worship run smoothly. To my surprise, several people around the table were nodding their heads. While making worship run smoothly is one of the things we DO, it isn't WHY we exist. I realized we had experienced mission drift. Our vision had leaked, and I knew if it had leaked for our staff team, it had leaked for our volunteers.

The Guest Connections team spent the next four months getting clarity on our vision. A book that was helpful to us in this process was Patrick Lencioni's *The Advantage*. We began by asking ourselves, *What do we do?* Once we'd answered that, we asked why and then why again, over and over, until we'd gotten to the reason behind everything that each of us does—the *why* that connected us together. We developed a renewed sense of how all our volunteers, from the seatback stuffers and Communion servers to our door greeters and ushers, help demonstrate radical hospitality. Worship flows smoothly as a by-product of what we do, but there is a much bigger why behind it. Lencioni writes: "Employees in every organization, and at every level, need to know that at the heart of what they do lies something grand and aspirational."[1] We reached a consensus on the vision that binds us together:

> Everything we do is done with the vision of creating interactions
> and environments that enable people to experience the love
> of God.

We do that by demonstrating radical hospitality. The *why* behind that? To build a Christian community where nonreligious and nominally religious people are becoming deeply committed Christians SO THAT people's lives are changed, churches are strengthened, and our community and the world are transformed.

These last two statements are our church's purpose and vision statement.

Following our re-visioning for our staff team, we were excited to begin recasting vision for our volunteers, to remind them of the why of their ministry and how it connects with the vision of the church.

Around the same time, we invited some secret shoppers to visit and help us gain a fresh perspective. They shared with us what they thought we did well, and then they identified some gaps they found. I encourage you to invite a friend or hire a secret shopper to review your spaces and events through a first-timer's eyes and share their observations and experience with you. They will undoubtedly notice at least one thing that you've not noticed or that you've stopped seeing. Take to heart the feedback they give.

Casting Vision and Developing Training

We developed a ninety-minute volunteer training that incorporated our clear vision and many of the secret shopper findings. We invited our key leaders to participate first and provide suggestions for making the workshop better. Because they helped shape the training, they felt a sense of ownership of the vision and a buy-in for the training. The final format for the training we developed includes the vision for radical hospitality that changes people's lives, the principles of hospitality, clear expectations for behavior, and examples and stories of how those are lived out in our ministries.

Start with Existing Teams

As you cast vision and develop training, we strongly recommend that you start with your existing teams. Don't just train new volunteers. If you add newly trained, highly motivated volunteers to a base that isn't living out radical hospitality, they'll be confused, and your vision will lose momentum. You know this to be true from your own experience: spend time with happy, hardworking people, and you are more likely to work hard and be happy. And nothing brings you down faster than hanging out with someone who complains all the time. Make sure your existing teams grasp and live out your vision, so they serve as role models for new volunteers. If you have volunteers who can't or won't support your vision, help them find a new place to serve. You want your volunteer teams to be comprised of people who share your vision because it resonates with who they are deep inside.

When we were ready, we started by inviting our existing volunteers to what we called our Volunteer Orientation Gathering. Perhaps your church is different, but at our church, people are more likely to attend a gathering than a training (and more likely to attend anything if food is involved). We had a few new recruits we invited, but it was especially important to us to share this time with our volunteers who had been serving in their roles for a long time. We asked our current volunteers to come and sit with new people, to get to know them so the new volunteers would feel comfortable when they arrived to serve.

Begin with Why

There are three components to the operation of any organization, including the church. First is *what* (the service it provides or the product it sells), second is *how* (the specific ways it delivers their product or service that differentiates it from others in the same field), and third is *why* (what the organization believes, the purpose behind its what and how). Most organizations focus their communication on what they do and how they do it.

Simon Sinek talks about the importance of communicating a compelling *why* in his book, *Start with Why*: "Very few people or companies can clearly articulate WHY they do WHAT they do....By WHY I mean what is your purpose, cause or belief? WHY does your company exist? WHY do you get out of bed every morning? And WHY should anyone care?"[2] Sinek explains that the *what* and the *how* connect to the part of our brain where rational and analytical thought is controlled. Rational thought and analysis don't influence behavior. We all know we should eat healthier foods and exercise more, but that knowledge doesn't automatically translate into new habits. The *why* connects to the part of the brain where feelings and behaviors reside, and that's what inspires and motivates us to action.

As we mentioned in chapter 1, the first step is to identify why your church exists—what your specific congregation's purpose is and what role your ministry plays in accomplishing that purpose. Lencioni writes, "So how does an organization go about figuring out why it exists? It starts by asking this question: 'How do we contribute to a better world?'"[3] It's not as easy as it sounds to identify your purpose, one that you're willing to stand behind for as long as your organization exists. Your true purpose doesn't change over time, though your method for achieving it might. In their book *Built to Last*, Jim Collins and Jerry I. Porras write: "When properly conceived, purpose is broad, fundamental, and enduring; a good purpose should serve to guide and inspire the organization for years, perhaps a century or more....Indeed, a visionary company continually pursues but never fully achieves or completes its purpose—like chasing the earth's horizon or pursuing a guiding star."[4]

Every year our team selects one book to study together, related to how we work together or the specific ministry we do. Over the last several years we've studied and discussed *The Advantage* (Patrick Lencioni), *Crucial Conversations, The New Gold Standard* (Joseph A. Michelli), *Be Our Guest* (Disney Institute), and *The Power of Moments* (Chip Heath and Dan Heath). Each of those books has helped us clarify and better articulate our *why* in a way that resonates with the heartbeat of our church.

Inspiring leaders recognize the importance of connecting with people's emotions, helping them see themselves as contributors to something bigger and more significant than themselves that taps into the deep-seated beliefs and values that resonate strongly with who they are. If you want to change or influence people's behavior—ultimately to change the culture of your congregation—you must connect with their emotions. Clarifying and communicating the *why* behind your purpose is the best way to do that. Compare these two ways to ask volunteers to help clean the worship space in between services:

> After the first worship service, make sure the worship space is clean for the next service. Pick up any stray bulletins or trash, set the sections for the second service. We want the space to look and feel ready for our guests.

Versus something more like this:

> We know many of our guests are coming to church with all sorts of questions, worries, and distractions on their minds. To help them transition from what's on their minds into a sacred space where they can encounter God and find peace, we want the worship

space to be clean and distraction free, so there's no barrier to them meeting God. Help us make that happen by straightening up your section after each service.

Jesus was very clear on his *why*, his mission, and it shaped everything he did: "The Human One came to seek and save the lost" (Luke 19:10).

It's the reason he stepped outside the lines of the law so many times. He took every opportunity he had to connect with people on the margins at a personal level, to remind them that God had not forgotten them and loved them just as they were, despite the societal norms of his day.

At Resurrection, our purpose, building a Christian community where nonreligious and nominally religious people are becoming deeply committed Christians, drives everything we do. It's the reason we talk about issues that matter to unchurched people; it's the reason we provide easy entry points and on-ramps for participation (and then raise the expectations for spiritual growth); and it's the reason we are unwaveringly committed to being outwardly focused.

One example of how this purpose provides clarity in decision-making happened in the late 2000s, when Richard Dawkins's book *The God Delusion* was released, and Pastor Adam decided to deliver a sermon series entitled "Conversations with an Atheist" to discuss and respond to the points in this book. He received many questions and not a few complaints. One note in particular said (I'm paraphrasing), "I don't care about what atheists think, and I think we ought to stick to teaching Scripture. I'm going to leave the church if you preach a sermon series on this book." Adam was able to respond graciously, because we are clear about our church's purpose, that we would be sorry to see this gentleman leave the church, but there are a number of excellent churches in Kansas City that would meet his needs. At Resurrection, we want to reach nonreligious and nominally religious people, and that means we're going to talk about the things they're talking about, preach into the issues that matter to them, and in the process, we hope to create an opening for the Holy Spirit to work in them. Clarity on your *why* helps you reach a faster yes and a more gracious no on any decision.

As we began to develop training for our volunteers, we knew our most important task was to share a compelling vision for the *why* behind their ministry role and the principles of radical hospitality, to inspire a clear sense of purpose that connected with them personally. We believed the best way to do that was through the power of sharing stories.

Use the Power of Stories to Bring Life to Your Vision

The best way to bring life to your vision comes from sharing stories, which are easier to remember than facts and figures, and connect actions with our emotions. Stories that move us have the power to change our behavior. Remember, we act on our emotions, not on facts. In *Made to Stick*, Chip and Dan Heath put it this way: "How do we get people to care about our ideas? We make them *feel* something....We are wired to feel things for people, not for abstractions."[5] Share stories that illustrate the impact your vision will have on the lives of real people if it's brought to fruition. By doing so, you connect your ideas to their emotions.

The authors go on to say that stories serve as mental practice for how we should behave in future situations: "Research has suggested that mental rehearsal can prevent people from relapsing into bad habits such as smoking, excessive drinking, or overeating."[6] Elite athletes often visualize their competitive event, all the way to seeing themselves accepting the prize. Public speakers visualize doing their presentation or talk and having it well-received. Many nutritionists ask clients to mentally rehearse holiday meals, or how they will eat on vacations in order to stay on track with their goals.

Think about how Jesus taught lessons using stories that related to his listeners' life experiences. In Luke 6:27, he says "But I say to you who are willing to hear: Love your enemies." That's a very clear direction, but it's an abstract idea. On the other hand, his parable in Luke 10 contains much more vivid language in story form, and was more likely to lead people to explore how they would behave if they were in a similar situation:

A legal expert stood up to test Jesus. "Teacher," he said, "what must I do to gain eternal life?"

Jesus replied, "What is written in the Law? How do you interpret it?"

He responded, "You must love the Lord your God with all your heart, with all your being, with all your strength, and with all your mind, and love your neighbor as yourself."

Jesus said to him, "You have answered correctly. Do this and you will live."

But the legal expert wanted to prove that he was right, so he said to Jesus, "And who is my neighbor?"

Jesus replied, "A man went down from Jerusalem to Jericho. He encountered thieves, who stripped him naked, beat him up, and left him near death. Now it just so happened that a priest was also going down the same road. When he saw the injured man, he crossed over to the other side of the road and went on his way. Likewise, a Levite came by that spot, saw the injured man, and crossed over to the other side of the road and went on his way. A Samaritan, who was on a journey, came to where the man was. But when he saw him, he was moved with compassion. The Samaritan went to him and bandaged his wounds, tending them with oil and wine. Then he placed the wounded man on his own donkey, took him to an inn, and took care of him. The next day, he took two full days' worth of wages and gave them to the innkeeper. He said, 'Take care of him, and when I return, I will pay you back for any additional costs.' What do you think? Which one of these three was a neighbor to the man who encountered thieves?"

Then the legal expert said, "The one who demonstrated mercy toward him."

Jesus told him, "Go and do likewise." (vv. 25-37)

Stories help us see ourselves in the narrative. Jesus's listeners would have been able to picture themselves coming across this injured man and would have wondered (mentally practiced, and hopefully pre-decided) how they would respond in a similar situation.

At Resurrection, we wanted to help our volunteers see themselves leading the way in our radical hospitality efforts, so we began to collect and record stories, capturing photos wherever possible. In the training we developed, we shared stories and images of how we saw them demonstrating hospitality with excellence and why it mattered. Our aim was to remind them of the eternal impact of first impressions. We painted a picture for our teams of the impact their acts of radical hospitality had on real people's lives and helped them understand the difference they make as individuals.

Our goal was to help them connect the dots between their ministry and people coming to faith, having their lives forever changed. It was aspirational and, we hoped, compelling. The feedback we've gotten on the training is that our volunteers leave feeling excited and motivated to act. Even longtime volunteers told us they felt a renewed sense of purpose. Following are a couple of stories we shared to help our volunteers see themselves living our vision for radical hospitality.

In April 2017, we had our first Easter in the new sanctuary. Bruce, one of our head ushers, served at every Sunday morning service that day. After the 11 a.m. service, the last of the morning, while he was cleaning up his section for the evening services, a family asked if he'd take their photo in front of the beautiful Easter flowers on the chancel. He readily agreed. When he finished, another family tapped him on the shoulder, and then another. A few minutes later he looked behind him, and there was a line back to the entrance to the sanctuary, waiting for Bruce to take their photos, which he did. Bruce stayed until 1:30 that afternoon, helping our guests capture a precious moment of their first Easter in our new sanctuary. Bruce and his wife probably had Easter plans of their own, but he went the extra mile to provide a great experience for our guests.

Another story we shared involves our shuttle drivers. We have a large campus to navigate, and sometimes guests have to park in the hinterlands, so we bought a couple of golf carts to offer rides to those who park far away from the building. One rainy day last summer, I came in for our 11 a.m. traditional service, which is our largest. Just as I got out of my car, one of the shuttles came by and offered a ride. I stepped in, and we started off. About that time a little guy, maybe seven years old, gets out of an SUV and flags us down. "We want a ride! We want a ride!" On the way to the building, the boy and his younger brother held on to the rails in front of their seat, saying "Vroom! Vroom! Whee!" when the shuttle driver took gentle *S* curves as he drove. We arrived at the door and as we walked in, the mom turned to me and said, "That's how we get them to church every week. We promise them a shuttle ride, and the drivers always make it fun."

We were transparent in our training, sharing examples of where we had fallen short as well as when we'd gotten it right. One important piece of advice—any story you share about a failing should either be universal—this often happens (with no names attached)—or it should be a story about yourself. Don't be afraid to be vulnerable. One story that I share is this:

In January one year we had a movie night in our sanctuary. We had planned for about seven hundred participants, but by the day of the event, we knew we'd be well over capacity. Somehow a local Christian radio station heard and was announcing over the air that we'd be showing the film for free that evening. The subject of the movie was a local Holocaust survivor who had been giving talks about hope and determination to local high schools, and she had a large local fan base.

Around 4 p.m., a teammate and I were frantically bagging popcorn for the attendees who would begin arriving soon when a man walked down the hallway; something about him made me uncomfortable. We greeted him, and he asked what kind of building we were in. He said he was just walking past and thought the building looked interesting, so he thought he'd come see what it was. We explained that we are a church, and we were just outside our sanctuary. When he asked if he could go inside, we told him, "Absolutely!" My teammate got him a brochure that described the building and the stained-glass window, and as he walked into the sanctuary, we went back to hastily preparing for the event.

A few minutes later he came out, we said goodbye, and he left. I admitted to my teammate within minutes that I felt like I'd missed an opportunity with that young man. I wished I had introduced myself, gotten his name, and made sure he felt welcomed. Instead, I was focused completely on the task in front of me and kind of worried that we should call security. I don't know if that man will ever come back to Resurrection, but I will never get another opportunity to make an excellent first impression, and that haunts me.

Repeat, Repeat, Repeat

Share your vision through stories and pictures over and over again. In *The Advantage*, Patrick Lencioni writes:

> The problem is that leaders confuse the mere transfer of information to an audience with the audience's ability to understand, internalize, and embrace the message that is being communicated. The only way for people to embrace a message is to hear it over a period of time, in a variety of different situations, and preferably from different people....Great leaders see themselves as Chief Reminding Officers as much as anything else.[7]

Since vision constantly leaks, to keep it alive you must continuously, repeatedly remind those you lead about the vision and, as we've said, stories and images are the most powerful way to do that. Ask people questions about their experiences, write them down, and share them frequently. We try to catch our people doing something right, and then share the story or a photo with the whole team. We want these principles to become a way of life for our people, for them to carry them forward into the community. Wherever your church is, large or small, it has a reputation in the community. Sharing stories, both good and bad, reminds your people of the impact their actions have wherever they go.

One story we've shared was about a woman who had exchanged terse words with another woman, a manager at a local business on a Saturday afternoon. She knew she had been kind of rude, but she was angry and still feeling frustrated when she got to church that evening. Then the pastor announced the stand-and-greet-time, and the woman reached out her hand...only to find the woman she was rude to earlier sitting right in front of her. She said it was so embarrassing and a bit of a wake-up call for her.

Another woman shared a story about shopping for our annual school supply drive at a local Target. She was chatting with the cashier as she checked out, and the cashier asked her if she attended Resurrection. When she replied yes, the cashier said to her, "I don't go to church, but if I ever did, I'd come to your church. I've had twenty people go through my line over the last few days buying school supplies for inner-city kids they'll never meet, and they were all the nicest people. That's the kind of church I'd want to go to."

These are very different stories, but both are the kinds of stories your people can imagine themselves in, and both serve to inspire people to be kind and extend hospitality not just at church, but wherever they go.

Make the Vision Concrete

We try to make the vision concrete in two ways: with stories that illustrate the vision with clear language as discussed above, and with tools that explicitly define the vision. Describe clearly the attitudes and behaviors you expect from your volunteers using volunteer position descriptions, concisely stated principles, and other ways of defining your expectations and aspirations. These practical tools with clear, concrete language make the vision well-defined and help people grasp abstract ideas more easily.

We developed some written tools to help our teams clearly understand what we are asking of them. Copies of these are available for
download at sharechurch.com. There are ministry position descriptions, which help us clarify the expectations for new volunteers by
defining their role. There is a volunteer covenant that we ask every
volunteer to sign, and we have a more extensive one for leaders,
as well.

The volunteer covenant outlines Resurrection's four distinctives.
These are the filters through which we ask our volunteers to make
decisions about what to do. First is Outward-Focused. We want our
words and actions to make nonreligious or nominally religious people
comfortable. Second is Hope-Radiating. Our words and actions should
create environments and interactions that enable people to experience
the love of Christ. Third is Thought-Provoking. We desire to share our
beliefs openly with others while being respectful, kind, and gentle
toward those who believe differently. Fourth is Bridge-Building. Our
desire is to say or do things that make it easy for guests to build
connections with the church and with other people. In our training, we
role-play these with a few common situations we see. Yes, it's awkward.
Everybody rolls their eyes, but it makes these expectations practical
and relatable. Finally, at the bottom, the covenant lists the expectations
for all volunteers regardless of the specific way they serve.

These concrete tools—the position description, the covenant, the
role-play—are helpful when you need to have a conversation with a
volunteer who isn't meeting expectations. Having those tools in place
and reviewing them with volunteers before they start serving enables
you to point back to them if a volunteer isn't working out. It makes
the conversation less about them as a person and more about the
expectations you have for anyone serving in ministry.

Create Visible and Tangible Reminders

Provide visible and tangible reminders of the value, principles,
and practice of radical hospitality. We give each volunteer a folded

business-sized card during training that outlines our principles. These principles are also framed and hanging on the walls of our volunteer gathering spaces. Every communication we have with a team is an opportunity to share training reminders with a few sentences or a brief video (shot on our phones) highlighting our expectations.

When our leaders send out their weekly email to volunteers, they include a snippet about one of the principles of radical hospitality, how that specific team lives into that topic, and the impact it has on those they meet. We try to vary the method of communication, so it doesn't become something they skip past.

Demonstrate Hospitality in Every Ministry

Make sure your volunteers and congregants see you demonstrate radical hospitality consistently throughout your ministries. If it is to permeate your culture, it has to be a value that flows from the top down and from the inside out. Hospitality isn't just a guest services function; it's the way church ought to operate. Every ministry should hold and demonstrate a high value of hospitality.

Encourage your people to demonstrate radical hospitality to each other. Our teams and our congregants have to first *experience* a great hospitality culture if we want them to reflect a great hospitality culture. It's great practice and soon it becomes the social norm of behavior. When your leaders, volunteers, and congregants have a common language around radical hospitality, the practice of it multiplies as they constantly "drip" the vision from one person to the next.

Will Mancini, a church consultant with the Auxano Group said in a presentation at Church of the Resurrection in April 2018: "Vision dripping is much more impactful than vision casting. Preaching or staff communication is vital, but constant dripping of vision from non-staff leader to leader to individual has ten times the impact," and that's a powerful thing.

Once your current volunteers are on board with the vision and living into your value of radical hospitality, you're ready to focus on recruiting new volunteers.

Recruiting

Recruiting volunteers is an ongoing process, and it can be challenging at times. There isn't a magic pill that will solve every recruiting problem. We've found that recruiting new volunteers requires utilizing a variety of means available to us. Some of the methods we've used here at Resurrection include making an announcement from the chancel during worship services, putting them up on the website, listing them in our newsletters, having sign-up tables outside our sanctuary, and posting them on social media.

The important thing to remember when using any recruitment method is that you must include an easy way for people to act on the invitation. If you print the need for volunteers in the bulletin, tell people who to contact and how. If it's an announcement as part of worship, ask people to fill out a card with contact information or raise their hands and have them meet you in the lobby afterward. Recently we've used technology and asked congregants to text SERVE to a number we've set up in advance, which automatically sends them a link to more information. If you are putting it in an email like a newsletter or note from the pastor, include a hyperlink to sign up. Ensure when you make the request that you create an easy way for people to act on it and then follow up in a timely manner!

Another way we have recruited volunteers is with signage. If we have a service with Communion and we need more servers, we have a sign out near the check-in table that says, "Communion Servers Still Needed." People who see the sign and want to help will stop and fill a need for that week—and often they become part of the regular team too. Our children's ministry does this too, placing a sign at a classroom door that says they need more parent volunteers for that class. Signs can be effective as long as there is someone close by to plug people in; a sign standing by itself is useless.

Another volunteer recruiting tool you may use is to partner with other ministries in your church. Partner with your student ministry team to plug students into serving roles or with dads from your men's ministry to provide childcare during a women's event. Our confirmation students have a service requirement to complete confirmation, and many of them enjoy it enough to continue serving long after they've been confirmed. Working with other ministries to recruit volunteers not only helps fill your open positions, but helps other ministries understand your needs and become ambassadors for filling them too.

Don't be afraid to use a little humor. Laughter can be a powerful tool. Our downtown location shot a video of the worship leader singing the 1970s Eric Carmen song "All by Myself," with images of the staff doing every volunteer role in an empty building. It closed with a slide that said, "We can't do it alone; we need you!" Similarly, at our Leawood location, we shot a video that showed Pastor Adam greeting a new family, filling every role from parking volunteer to barista in the coffee shop to worship leader, ending with the parents in the family saying, "Maybe we should volunteer."

Video can be an especially useful way to capture the imagination of your guests. Videos allow you to show the story of what you are inviting them to do. Moreover, it can be an opportunity to feature testimonies from those who are directly benefiting from the serving role you are working to fill. Stories and pictures are compelling tools that we should be using to recruit new volunteers.

Finally, the most effective way to recruit more volunteers is through a personal invitation. When someone hears "you would be great at this," it's hard to ignore. When you notice a trait or skill that would pair well with a serving role, let that person know. Encourage your current volunteers to invite their friends to serve with them once to try it out. This allows you to multiply this principle over and over. In addition, they will be inviting new people to serve alongside them, helping to build community on your teams. If your volunteers are inspired, understand the vision for their ministry and how it impacts the lives of real people, AND they're having fun, they'll *want* to invite their friends to join them.

Onboarding

Once you have recruited new volunteers, you need to make sure that you onboard and orient them with clearly defined expectations. To make sure a new volunteer truly understands the expectations, we give them a position description first and then invite them to shadow an experienced volunteer. We are very intentional about matching the new person up with one of our best volunteers, so they have an excellent role model. Tempting as it may be to plug the hole we have by just filling it right away with a new volunteer, we need to make sure we are taking the time to do it in a way that honors the new volunteer, the existing team, and the people they will be serving.

New volunteers should be oriented to the greater purpose and vision of the ministry they are serving in as well as to the specific role they are filling. Both parts of that statement are equally important. When we only do the first one, we leave volunteers with a grand vision but little in the way of practical knowledge. When we skip the first and only train for the role, we miss out on sharing how this role works within the grander vision we are trying to create. Both need to be done well and, whenever possible, before the new volunteer starts serving on a regular basis. Onboarding new volunteers well is the first step in making them long-term volunteers, if not lifers.

After onboarding, it's important to continue supporting volunteers by providing all the tools and resources needed to live fully into the expectations we have laid out. Every serving role we have will need different tools to help it succeed.

For our volunteers who come in during the week to refill and refresh our seatbacks, we provide a kit with seatback supplies (pens, sermon note cards, offering envelopes) for each of them to pick up that easily lets them grab and go. For our volunteers who work at our Connection Point (our information desk) there is a notebook with information that gets updated every week that makes it easy for them to find answers for guests' questions. Communion servers get an instruction card each time they serve.

Each of these provides tools that are needed and appreciated by our volunteers. When a team member shows up to serve and they can't find the resources or information that they need to serve well, it causes confusion and frustration. When we anticipate their needs and provide for them it not only makes their service experience run smoothly, it's a delight for our volunteers. One way to make sure you are providing the necessary tools is to make sure you are checking in with team members regularly and asking the question, "Do you need anything?"

Finally, helping a new volunteer stick comes down to modeling the actions and attitudes you expect—it starts from the top. One day, Pastor Adam was walking briskly down the stairs in our Commons area, clearly headed for another meeting, when a woman entered our doors juggling a casserole and some bags. She was headed for one of our Building Better Moms classes. Without hesitation, Adam switched direction and walked toward her. He took the casserole from her and walked back upstairs with her to the class she was going to. A few minutes later he headed back down the stairs, striding quickly to his next meeting. Adam is a busy guy around here and it would have been easy, even justifiable, for him to have just continued on to his original destination. Instead, he noticed this woman struggling and made time to help her out. That's modeling radical hospitality from the top down. We need to remember that people are always watching to see what we will do. Make sure that you are modeling what you are teaching.

Leading Change

Recruiting and training volunteers takes time and effort to do well. It's a constant process, at least for us. That's one reason it can be especially hard when we realize that a change is needed in one of our ministries. We recognize that it can be hard and painful for our volunteers. Making a change in a ministry will be difficult for us as leaders too. Change is just hard. It brings out all kinds of fears on the part of our volunteers: *Does this mean I've been doing something wrong? What if I can't do this new thing? How will this change impact me? What if I'm not needed anymore?* For ministry leaders, other kinds of fears come up: *What if I can't move this forward? What if my volunteers get angry or won't do it? Will this be all-consuming?*

Change is important, nonetheless. We all recognize this. There are times when we look at our teams and can clearly see that something needs to change. Sometimes the change comes as part of living into a new model of ministry; it's something we feel inspired to do. Other times we just recognize that a ministry team has run its course and it's time to bring it to an end in order to do something new. Sometimes it comes out of desperation when we find ourselves in need of a course correction. If you are reading this book, it's likely that you are considering a change. You want to make hospitality a priority, want to take the practical steps to live into this vision. It will require change, and maybe the change will be hard. Whatever the specific reason for the change you need to make, there are a few things that you can do to help minimize the pain and pave the way for new things.

First of all, realize that we all resist change we didn't initiate, so don't take any resistance to change personally. Typically, it's the small minority of vocal critics of any change that make a transition challenging, but eventually, the vast majority of people will get behind and support a change they understand.

The most important task in implementing any change in ministry is to make sure we explain well why the change is needed to our volunteers. Why should they do something differently if the current process seems to work okay and is comfortable for them? Every person needs something a little different to be okay with change, but everyone needs to understand the why. If we don't communicate the need for change well, we can't expect our volunteers to embrace it. We will probably need to communicate it more than once, and we should introduce the change in person.

Gather your team and explain the change and why it is needed. Help them see your vision for what could be, and how the status quo isn't going to get your church or your ministry where it needs to be.

Give time for questions and concerns. Every change means a new thing replaces something that will be lost. The loss could be expertise, if things have been done the same way for years. It could be confidence, if someone's not comfortable with the new practice. It could be old relationships, if they're being asked to serve with new people. Taking the time to listen to people's concerns gives them the space to grieve the loss of what was. It gives you the opportunity to acknowledge that they will lose some things with the change even as they start something new.

In 2018, we relaunched a service in our newly remodeled Foundry Hall that previously happened in our Student Center. The original service (called Vibe) had been combined with another service in our sanctuary during the renovation of the Foundry Hall space.

As we began planning the relaunch of this service (newly named Foundry), we recognized that we needed to train the volunteers who had been serving at Vibe to serve in a new way. The new space itself was so different that their previous way of serving would simply not suffice. In this case, the biggest felt loss was a casualness in how volunteers were assigned to serve. The new space is much larger and much more spread out, so many more volunteers are required. The space also has exterior doors where outside greeters were needed, which we didn't have in the previous space.

We recognized that taking the time to listen to our volunteers' concerns and acknowledging that there was a bit of grief over "what used to be" allowed us to move forward with clarity and buy-in. If we had skipped this step, instituting change would have been much harder. It still wasn't perfect, but the vast majority of the volunteers were able to understand and embrace the new way of serving. Often simply listening and acknowledging, without taking concerns or criticisms personally, can help with the process of change.

Sometimes implementing change takes a lot more work. In April of 2018, the secret shoppers we had asked to evaluate our hospitality delivered their report. Somehow, gradually over time, our greeters had stopped greeting people from outside our doors and moved to greeting them inside our doors. This is a great example of vision leaking and of our team losing awareness by being too familiar with what we were seeing. We were aware that greeters were greeting inside, and knew that ideally they would stand outside. But the secret shopper report created a real sense of urgency for us, showing us just how important it was to lead them to start greeting outside again. The secret shoppers showed us pictures of the blank doors that greeted our guests as they arrived for worship. It didn't offer a warm welcome. We needed to act quickly to get our greeters to move back outside the doors to offer radical hospitality to everyone as they arrived.

An important fact about our greeter teams at that time was that most had been serving in this role for years, and the average age of our greeters was well over sixty. That's not a bad thing; we're grateful for people of all ages who serve. But we recognized that making this change was going to be difficult. Asking our greeters to step outside in the elements was going to be hard for some of them and impossible for others.

We spent some time drafting the language around the need for the change and how we planned to implement it. Thankfully the weather would be moderate when we hoped to get started. Our first step was to share the news with our Head Greeters who lead our teams to make sure they were ready to lead through the change.

And then we let our greeter teams know. In the first month we lost about 30 percent of our greeter teams and over the next few months we lost another 20 percent. In total, we lost about half of our team. Internally, we called this the Great Greeter Revolt of 2018. The truth is that no matter how well you explain why the change is needed, some people will not be able to make the change with you. Be prepared for it to get worse before it gets better.

Many of our greeters still had a heart to greet our guests but just physically couldn't do the task. For some of our frailer volunteers, the doors to our sanctuary were quite difficult to open, especially with a strong wind working against them. We worked hard to find creative ways to still allow them to serve, like greeting outside or inside the sanctuary. We also encouraged our greeters to use their best judgment. On really cold days we ask them to take turns greeting outside. One will greet outside for a bit while the other greets at the inner doors, and then they switch. Others simply weren't interested in serving in the new way, so we offered to help find them another serving role in the church. While it was difficult to lose so many volunteers, we also recognized that we were also saying goodbye to some volunteers whose attitudes didn't line up with our vision of radical hospitality. We learned that the volunteers who remained now fully embraced their serving role and understood the need to greet our guests from outside. It also means that as we recruit to refill this team, any new volunteer will know exactly what is expected.

Just as it's really important to make sure that your volunteers have all the necessary tools to serve with you, you can acknowledge their needs and their sacrifice with what you provide for them. Having our greeters serve out in the hot sun in the summer is a big ask. There is no shade on the west side of our sanctuary, and the summer temperatures are often in the nineties, so we provide sunglasses and cold bottles of water for them. In the spring and fall we get some very wet weekends, so we provide umbrellas for them to use. In the winter it can get bitterly cold, and we provide extra gloves for anyone who forgets theirs, along with hand warmers. We offer hot cocoa in the meeting room for them to grab after they are done greeting and are on their way into worship. Each of these tools not only provides what they need to do the job, but also communicates that we recognize that what they are doing is difficult and we appreciate them. We take every opportunity to share with them positive feedback that we get from guests and when we "catch" them doing a great job. This helps keep the vision front and center for them and inspires them to show radical hospitality.

When done with excellence, radical hospitality can be truly life-changing. Early on New Year's Day in 2016, Joan, who serves in our café, was by herself preparing coffee for worship. A woman came in who had obviously been crying. She told Joan she somehow felt drawn to our church and was there to find her God. She apologized, and said she knew she shouldn't be there, because she was Muslim. Joan told her that everyone was welcome there and walked her over to our Firestone Chapel, where she could pray in privacy and peace as people began to arrive for worship. What Joan didn't know until two years later was that Farrah had attempted suicide the night before she came in and was welcomed by Joan.

In February of 2018, we invited congregants to come in and write their prayers on the sheetrock as we were remodeling what would become our fellowship space—the Foundry Hall. Farrah insisted that her prayer needed to be written on the new café wall instead. Here is the note she wrote on the café wall in the new Commons:

> Lord, thank you so much for saving my life on New Year's Eve 2015. Thank you so much for giving my life back to me, and putting me on the right path. Thank you for guiding me to come to COR and make all these friends and thank you for your ongoing support and protection through everyone and every particle of this church coming to me and my children. Please let me be a good follower of Jesus. Please Lord hold my hand; don't let me fall again, as a Muslim, as a Christian, or as a human. Thank you, God, for everything, for all your blessings to me. —Farrah
>
> P.S. It all started from the old café at COR and a beautiful lady named Joan.

The work we do, the hospitality we strive for, as volunteers, lay staff, or clergy, can and does change lives. Whether you serve in Operations, Worship Arts, Communications, or Hospitality, whether you serve with children or with the elderly, the ministry you do matters. Please don't ever forget that, and don't let your volunteer teams forget it, either.

CHAPTER CHALLENGE

1. Reflect on why radical hospitality matters to you. What is the why behind this vision for your personally? for your church?

2. Write down how you currently share a vision for excellent hospitality with your volunteer teams and congregants. How can you communicate that clearly and consistently using stories that touch their emotions?

3. What is the most important thing for your current and potential new volunteers to know from *The Art of Hospitality*? What tools and resources can you provide to make it easy for them to succeed?

4. Invite someone to serve as a secret shopper for your church, and report to you on their observations and experience. What is working well in your church when it comes to hospitality? What could be improved to enhance the guest experience?

10

EQUIPPING THE CONGREGATION

DEBI NIXON

It is our hope that as you have read this book, you have discovered ideas to help you develop practices where guests receive exceptional and consistent hospitality in your ministry context. And it is our hope that you have seen the value of dependable systems to help you achieve this goal.

Yet, creating better systems will not make the difference.

The difference is the attitude and heart of the leader. The difference is the attitude and heart of the volunteer. The difference is the attitude and heart of the congregation who commits to go above and beyond to love and care for others. This attitude and heart reflect a church whose culture declares that hospitality is a nonnegotiable value.

When hospitality is a value, it opens all people up to the work of God. A powerful ministry of hospitality not only serves your guests, but it inspires and disciples the entire congregation. When a congregation is inspired and transformed, a community is changed.

While the last chapter focused on creating a culture of hospitality by training and equipping volunteers serving in hospitality roles, that is only half of the equation. The other half is the rest of our congregation. A congregation that shares and models the values you place on hospitality is just as important as the committed volunteers who welcome your guests. It is highly likely a visitor will first encounter a congregant before one of the trained volunteers. One inhospitable congregant could offset the hundreds of other touchpoints of radical hospitality you have in place. It shouldn't, but it will.

Your culture of hospitality will be healthy or unhealthy depending on what you tolerate and allow to happen. Churches who value hospitality intentionally work to build and maintain the culture with an unwavering commitment to excellence.

In organ transplants, it is not uncommon for the body's own immune system to reject the new organ, even though the body needs it. You may experience this same type of rejection as you begin to introduce change within a longstanding organization. However, with careful planning as vision is cast for a new set of expectations, principles, and processes, the church body will gradually adapt and begin to accept the changes just like the body with careful planning and monitoring will accept a new organ.

Very little happens at Church of the Resurrection by happenstance. Even the smallest details matter. As you have already read, this value of excellence is reflected in the commitment we put into planning and execution in every area from ministry to children, to welcome in the parking lot, to the cleanliness of our bathrooms. We are not perfect and don't always get it right, but we are committed to evaluation, feedback, and making changes for the better. In weekly meetings, we talk about what is going well, determine if there are ways to improve, and recall our values as a reminder that this is why we exist.

You may have heard some in the congregation say, "It's good enough." But good enough won't compel others to give the church a try. "Good enough" undermines the amazing mission God is calling you to. Ministry requires hard work and constant effort. In dying organizations, "good enough" quickly becomes mediocrity where predictability and comfort sneak into the seat of transformative mission.

Transformative congregations pursue excellence and a "whatever it takes" spirit that resists the temptation to turn inward, becoming comfortable and settled.

As the reader of this book, no matter your role in the church—laity or clergy, paid staff or volunteer, worship leader or nursery worker— you have an important role to cast vision constantly, set the example, and call the congregation to move beyond their comfort zone to do whatever it takes to extend hospitality. The leader must continually set an expectation of hospitality and model it. Just as the leader must keep the vision in front of the volunteers, the leader must also continually remind the whole congregation of the *why*.

A couple described their first visit to our church back when it was still meeting in a funeral home. Because they did not know anyone, this couple felt anxious before arriving. Yet the moment they arrived, there was a greeter in the parking lot who extended a warm smile and greeting that eased any fear. Recognizing they were new, the greeter personally walked with them into the church, helping them check their two toddlers into the nursery. The greeter then took them to the sanctuary and introduced them to an usher who helped them find a seat. Then, in the midst of worship, the couple realized the parking greeter was the senior pastor. And at that moment, they knew they had found a church home.

When you have leaders who not only cast vision but model the vision by the way they lead and live when no one else is looking, great things will happen, and others will follow. Our senior pastor Adam Hamilton has set the example for hospitality from the beginning, and he continues to do it to this day. He picks up trash, he wipes down countertops, he parks the farthest away, he notices people. And he sets the example not only by his practices, but the message of hospitality is shared in his preaching, teaching, storytelling, and weekly communi- cation to the congregation.

Staying on Course

Several years ago, one of our congregants was overheard asking a visitor to move because the visitor had "sat in their seats." When Adam was made aware of this occurrence, the very next weekend from the pulpit he told the congregation that this is not the kind of church we are; we don't have reserved seats. He shared his expectation this was to never happen again. He was bold and direct, yet compassionate as he reminded the church of our mission and purpose. We don't want to have any barriers that would prevent someone from encountering Christ, but instead we want to be a bridge.

Don't miss this: Adam was willing to address the situation, initiating an uncomfortable conversation with the entire congregation. It would have been easier to simply dismiss the incident, reducing the risk of upsetting anyone, especially if that someone was a significant donor or church board member. Remember culture is not only what you create, but what you allow to happen. An inwardly focused congregation is a visible sign of unhealthy behavior that has been tolerated far too long.

During the launch of one of our locations, the volunteers were trained in the practices of hospitality. Yet, it took months for the practices to be implemented. Each weekend, volunteer greeters migrated inside the doors where it was more comfortable and easier to see their friends rather than being outside the doors to welcome guests as they arrived. Eventually the migration ceased, and they simply just started there. It might have been easier to ignore the behavior and simply be glad we had volunteers close to a door, any door, to greet someone. But this practice did not match our value of hospitality, and it required the leader to determine a way to address it.

At first the leader would give a kind verbal instruction to greet outside the doors. "Hey greeters, thanks for being here. Just a reminder, please greet outside on the front sidewalk and open the doors for guests when they arrive." But bad habits are hard to break, and while the volunteers may have heard the instruction, over time they would migrate inside again. Let's be honest. It only takes the one volunteer who moves inside to start the migration where the rest would follow.

So, a new tactic was employed.

One of our leaders would arrive each week and take their place outside without saying a word. After a few weeks, the scheduled volunteers started noticing and asked if they could help outside. Within a few months of repeating this behavior, each volunteer spot was filled by volunteers who stood outside the doors simply because it was modeled for them.

Training is important, but for it to stick, it must be repetitively modeled. And that modeling affects not only the volunteers but also the rest of the congregation and, eventually, the whole culture of your church.

Changing Hearts and Minds

While coaching a church in a rural area, one of the action steps we recommended was to implement a parking lot ministry where a volunteer was present in the parking lot to greet guests when they arrived. There was initial resistance because the church had not welcomed any visitors in quite some time, so having a volunteer in the parking lot to greet the members seemed unnecessary. We encouraged the church to start the parking lot ministry as "practice" for when the first visitor would arrive, knowing from our own experience that something transformational would occur.

And it did. The simple experience of being greeted by a person weekly in the parking lot began to change the hearts and behaviors of the members. Everyone loves a smile, a welcome, a handshake. And eventually when a visitor did arrive, each of the members was prepared to extend radical hospitality that was not coerced or perfunctory. It flowed from transformed hearts.

A participant at one of our Art of Hospitality Conferences shared her church's experience of "going above and beyond" by adding greeters to all entrances in addition to the main entrance. One of those entrances was a seldom used handicap entrance. She told us, "It was long overdue for us to add a greeter at this entrance. It was not only appreciated by our valued elderly members but has been a blessing for those serving at that door who now realize that showing love to others in this greeter role uplifts the heart of the greeter as well as those they assist. And it doesn't even cost anything but time, so no budget battles to contend with. Yippee!"

When the hearts of the congregation become transformed, amazing things happen!

Earlier in the book we discussed the important role that first impressions play in determining the actions of guests. When the entire congregation values hospitality, they commit to impressions that demonstrate how much the church really cares. And this means that we must equip and expect everyone to deliver these favorable first impressions on a consistent basis. Each person in the congregation must envision that they might be the only contact a guest has with the church. What impression will they leave?

One idea to equip the congregation for radical hospitality is to provide them with simple resources. Each congregant at Church of the Resurrection is provided with a pocket testament with the hope that they will not only read it but pray that they will have the opportunity to give it away. It is a nonthreatening way for the congregation to be prepared to surprise someone and share God's love. Pastor Adam shares about an experience he had on a plane where a flight attendant saw him reading his pocket testament and began asking questions. They talked during the flight, and as he was deplaning, he handed her his pocket testament. That small, unexpected act is an example of hospitality.

We also worked with a promotional company to have a small coin printed called a Kindness Coin. Each congregant is given a kindness coin to place in their pocket, with an encouragement to demonstrate one act of radical hospitality or kindness each day, moving the coin from one pocket to the next as a reminder.

While the focus of this book has been on the hospitality within the church, that same value must be lived out in our daily lives. What if we offered these same practices of radical hospitality beyond the church building—in our workplace, at school, at a restaurant, or shopping? When we open our eyes to see others around us and welcome them into our lives, we are welcoming in Jesus. If we are willing to open our eyes and our hearts, we recognize opportunities to be the light of Christ everywhere! All too often we lead secure and comfortable lives, when God is calling us to risk discomfort to bring people hope and healing. As people who have been transformed by the living Christ, our only response must be to share this same love and hospitality with all we encounter. That could include those beside us in the line at the grocery store, the customer service person on the phone, the referee at our child's soccer game, the barista who makes our coffee, our spouse, our children, or anyone else we might encounter. The Kindness Coin helps as a daily reminder.

Ambassadors for Christ

When looking for the best in class of creating an exceptional guest experience, few businesses or churches have ever done it better than the Magic Kingdom. Creating an exceptional guest experience is the foundation of the culture at Disney.

In the book *The Experience*, authors Bruce Loeffler and Brian T. Church share Disney's focus and intentionality on equipping ambassadors to be a part of the mission. The word *ambassador* was carefully chosen, coming from Latin words meaning to "go on a mission."[1] The authors describe the mission as what happens when an experience that is valued and shared both internally and externally is cultivated. The mission is to empower others to be conduits of the experience in Disney's kingdom and to go out and share the story.

Disney knows that ambassadors must be developed. We must be developing our congregation to be ambassadors of the good news.

The church's mission is to be ambassadors of a kingdom more majestic than the Magic Kingdom of Disney. We are ambassadors for God's kingdom work. We are to be witnesses to God's redemptive work in the world, with the greatest story in the world to share! In John 3:16 we read, "God so loved the world that he gave his only Son, so that everyone who believes in him won't perish but will have eternal life."

God has chosen us, the church, to be conduits, ambassadors to share the story of God's love not just in word, but by our actions and deeds toward others. We are loved by God, we are redeemed by God. When we develop a lifestyle of hospitality, it becomes a way to share what Christ has done in our lives with others.

It is a way for others to not only hear us talking about this love, but see it, experience it for themselves, and feel drawn to it.

We opened in chapter 1 with the statement that we both love the mission of the church and we truly believe Jesus is the hope of the world. The mission of the church at its best throughout the centuries has been an outward mission focused on sharing the love Jesus has for the world, with the world. That is why this matters!

As a congregation, each person must be outward facing, humble, and hospitable to all. We hope this book has provided a new vision and practical ideas of what is possible when a church is transformed into a place that consistently extends hospitality to all.

The Lord's Prayer is a powerful kingdom vision prayer. When we pray it, we recognize God is inviting us as conduits, as ambassadors to move beyond our own comfort to help fulfill the kingdom mission on earth.

Practicing radical hospitality is an art. It requires the conscious use of skill and experience shaped by the radical hospitality we have received from Jesus.

When our church, our congregation is truly transformed by this radical hospitality, we can't help but welcome the stranger. And in this, we join God's kingdom mission.

It is time to start a movement where God can do great, miraculous things through us and through the church.

Let us pray:

Our Father, who art in heaven,
hallowed be thy name.
Thy kingdom come,
thy will be done on earth as it is in heaven.
Give us this day our daily bread.
And forgive us our trespasses,
as we forgive those who trespass against us.
And lead us not into temptation,
but deliver us from evil.
For thine is the kingdom, and the power, and the glory,
forever. Amen.[2]

CHAPTER CHALLENGE

1. Where has "good enough" mentality snuck into your culture versus a spirit of "whatever it takes"? Name two to three action steps to help your congregation remember the "why."

2. What does it mean to be ambassadors for Christ? What role does hospitality play?

3. As a leader, what are you committed to doing to ensure hospitality is maintained as a high value of the way you do ministry at your church?

4. What resources can you provide your congregation to equip them to live out this value of radical hospitality not only at the church, but in their personal lives as well?

NOTES

1. INWARD VERSUS OUTWARD CHURCHES

1   Thom S. Rainer, "The 10 Warning Signs of an Inwardly Obsessed Church," thomrainer.com, May 2, 2012. https://churchanswers.com/blog/the_inwardly_obsessed_church_10_warning_signs/.

2   Thom S. Rainer, "Four Major Ways Pastors Hinder Church Revitalization," thomrainer.com, October 29, 2015. https://www.christianpost.com/news/pastors-hinder-church-revitalization.html.

2. WHY HOSPITALITY MATTERS

1   Tyler Schmall, "This Is Exactly How Long You Have to Make a Good First Impression," *New York Post*, December 14, 2018, https://nypost.com/2018/12/14/this-is-exactly-how-long-you-have-to-make-a-good-first-impression/.

2   Karla Starr, "The Science of First Impressions," *Psychology Today*, February 8, 2013, www.psychologytoday.com/us/blog/the-science-luck/201302/the-science-first-impressions.

3   Jill Bremer, "Seven Minutes and Counting," in *Fusion: Turning First-Time Guests into Fully-Engaged Members of Your Church*, eds. Nelson Searcy and Jennifer Dykes Henson (Grand Rapids: Baker, 2007), 49.

4   Robert Schnase, *Five Practices of Fruitful Congregations* (Nashville: Abingdon Press, 2007), 21, 20.

5   Danny Franks, *People Are the Mission: How Churches Can Welcome Guests Without Compromising the Gospel* (Grand Rapids: Zondervan, 2018), 64.

3. THE PRINCIPLES OF HOSPITALITY

1   John Pavlovitz, *A Bigger Table: Building Messy, Authentic, and Hopeful Spiritual Community* (Louisville: Westminster John Knox, 2017), 72.

2   Jill Bremer, "Seven Minutes and Counting," 49; Schmall, "This Is Exactly How Long You Have to Make a Good First Impression."

3   Chip Heath and Dan Heath, *The Power of Moments: Why Certain Experiences Have Extraordinary Impact* (New York: Simon & Schuster, 2017), 55-56.

4   Amy G. Oden, *God's Welcome: Hospitality for a Gospel-Hungry World* (Cleveland: Pilgrim, 2008), 15.

4. CREATING A DIGITAL FRONT DOOR

1   "Internet/Broadband Fact Sheet," Pew Research Center, June 12, 2019, www.pewresearch.org/internet/fact-sheet/internet-broadband /#smartphone-dependency-over-time.

2   Carey Nieuwhof, "5 Disruptive Church Trends That Will Rule 2019," CareyNieuwhof.com, https://careynieuwhof.com/5-disruptive-church -trends-that-will-rule-2019/.

5. PROVIDING AN EXCELLENT IN-PERSON EXPERIENCE

1   Rich Birch, "5 Emotions First-Time Guests Feel When They Arrive at Your Church," unSeminary Podcast, November 6, 2018, https://unseminary .com/5-emotions-first-time-guests-feel-when-they-arrive-at-your-church/.

2   Andy Stanley, *Deep & Wide: Creating Churches Unchurched People Love to Attend* (Grand Rapids: Zondervan, 2012), 210.

6. CREATING AN EXCELLENT ONLINE EXPERIENCE

1   Alarming Average Screen Time Statistics (2024), https://explodingtopics .com/blog/screen-time-stats.

2   David Kinnaman, *Carey Nieuwhof Leadership Podcast* ep.623, Jan 9, 2024.

3   https://twitter.com/JonAcuff/status/309030566039273473.

4   Stanley, 284.

7. INTENTIONAL FOLLOW-UP

1   "Guest Follow-Up: Why It Matters and Why It's Not Happening," Faith Perceptions, November 14, 2016, https://faithperceptionsblog .com/2016/11/14/guest-follow-up-why-it-matters-and-why-its-not -happening/.

2   Tony Morgan, "Visitor Retention: Is Your Church Keeping Its Guests?" Tony Morgan Live, December 2, 2014, https://theunstuckgroup.com /visitor-retention-church-keeping-guests/.

3   Bill Easum, "How to Grow a Small Church," The Effective Church Group, 2007, https://effectivechurch.com/how-to-grow-a-small-church/.

4   Heath and Heath, *The Power of Moments,* 106-10.

5   Adam Hamilton, *The Walk: Five Essential Practices of the Christian Life* (Nashville: Abingdon Press, 2019).

8. SAFETY AND SECURITY HOSPITALITY

1   "Serious Violence at Places of Worship in the U.S.—Looking at the Numbers," https://www.dolanconsultinggroup.com/news/serious-violence-at-places-of-worship-in-the-u-s-looking-at-the-numbers/.

2   "The Power of Hello Guide for Houses of Worship," https://www.cisa.gov/sites/default/files/publications/The%20Power%20of%20Hello%20Guide%20for%20Houses%20of%20Worship_508.pdf.

3   "Cybersecurity & Infrastructure Security Agency (CISA):Resources & Tools," https://www.cisa.gov/resources-tools/resources/power-hello-houses-worship-guide.

9. CREATING A CULTURE OF HOSPITALITY

1   Patrick M. Lencioni, *The Advantage: Why Organizational Health Trumps Everything Else in Business* (San Francisco: Jossey-Bass, 2012), 82.

2   Simon Sinek, *Start with Why: How Great Leaders Inspire Everyone to Take Action* (New York: Penguin, 2009), 39.

3   Lencioni, 85.

4   Jim Collins and Jerry I. Porras, *Built to Last: Successful Habits of Visionary Companies* (New York: Harper Business, 1994), 10-11.

5   Chip Heath and Dan Heath, *Made to Stick: Why Some Ideas Survive and Others Die* (New York: Random House, 2007), 17-18.

6   Heath and Heath, *Made to Stick*, 213.

7   Lencioni, *The Advantage*, 142-43.

10. EQUIPPING THE CONGREGATION

1   Bruce Loeffler and Brian T. Church, *The Experience: The 5 Principles of Disney Service and Relationship Excellence* (Hoboken, NJ: John Wiley & Sons, 2015), 5.

2   "The Lord's Prayer," *The United Methodist Hymnal* (Nashville: The United Methodist Publishing House, 1989), 895.